Practising Theory and
Reading Literature

By the same author

English Verse Satire, 1590–1765, Allen & Unwin (1978)
Criticism and Objectivity, Allen & Unwin (1984)
The Poems of John Oldham, co-editor with Harold Brooks, Clarendon Press (1987)
Masterguide: John Dryden, Absalom and Achitophel, Penguin (1986)
The Theory of Criticism from Plato to the Present, Longman (1988)
A Reader's Guide to Contemporary Literary Theory, Harvester Press (1985; 2nd edn, 1989)

Practising Theory and Reading Literature

An Introduction

Raman Selden

Professor of English Literature
University of Lancaster

Harvester Wheatsheaf

New York   London   Toronto   Sydney   Tokyo

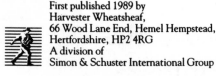

First published 1989 by
Harvester Wheatsheaf,
66 Wood Lane End, Hemel Hempstead,
Hertfordshire, HP2 4RG
A division of
Simon & Schuster International Group

Printed and bound in Great Britain by
Billing and Sons Ltd, Worcester

British Library Cataloguing in Publication Data

Selden, Raman
    Practising theory and reading literature
    1. Literature. Criticism
    I. Title
    8010.'95

    ISBN 0–7108–1146–2
    ISBN 0–7108–1158–6 Pbk

1 2 3 4 5   93 92 91 90 89

Contents

Preface

I am grateful to Harvester Wheatsheaf for suggesting and encouraging this book. I am much indebted to those colleagues at Lancaster University whose collaboration in the teaching of the theory and practice of criticism has kept me on my toes. I would like to thank especially Alison Easton, Michael Wheeler, David Carroll, Tony Sharpe, Robin Jarvis and Keith Hanley who have made helpful comments on individual chapters of the book. A particularly warm thank-you is due to Richard Dutton and Peter Widdowson who made penetrating observations on the entire manuscript.

Acknowledgements

Grateful acknowledgement is made to the following for permission to quote material in copyright:

Adcock, Fleur, 'The Ex-Queen among the Astronomers' from Selected Poems (1983). Reprinted by permission of Oxford University Press.

Heller, Joseph, an extract from Catch 22 (1955). Reprinted by permission of Joseph Heller and Jonathan Cape and Candida Donadio & Associates, copyright © 1955, 1961 by Joseph Heller.

Lawrence, D. H., an extract from 'The White Stocking', The Collected Short Stories, vol. I. Copyright 1933 by the Estate of D. H. Lawrence. Copyright renewed © 1961 by Angelo Ravagli and C. M. Weekley, Executors of the Estate of Frieda Lawrence Ravagli. All rights reserved. Reprinted by permission of Viking Penguin, Inc.

Lessing, Doris, an extract from Memoirs of a Survivor (1974). Copyright © 1974 by The Octagon Press; reprinted by permission of Alfred A. Knopf, Inc.

Mailer, Norman, an extract from An American Dream (1965). Reprinted by permission of André Deutsch Ltd and The Scott Meredith Literary Agency.

Orton, Joe, an extract from Loot (1967). Used by permission of Methuen London and Grove Press, a division of Wheatland Corporation.

Pinter, Harold, an extract from The Homecoming (1965). Used by permission of Methuen London and Grove Press, a division of Wheatland Corporation.

Raine, Craig, 'A Martian Sends a Postcard Home' from *A Martian Sends a Postcard Home* (1979). Reprinted by permission of Oxford University Press.

Rich, Adrienne, 'Planetarium'. All efforts have been made to trace the copyright holder. Grateful acknowledgement is made.

Smart, Christopher, an extract from *Jubilate Agno* in *The Poetical Works of Christopher Smart* (1980), vol. I (edited by Karina Williamson). Reprinted by permission of Oxford University Press.

Stevens, Wallace, 'A High-Toned Old Christian Woman', from *The Collected Poems of Wallace Stevens*. Reprinted by permission of Faber and Faber Ltd. Copyright 1923 and renewed 1951 by Wallace Stevens. Reprinted from *The Collected Poems of Wallace Stevens*, by permission of Alfred A. Knopf, Inc.

Williams, Tennessee, an extract from *The Glass Menagerie*. Copyright 1945 by Tennessee Williams and Edwina D. Williams and renewed 1973 by permission of Random House, Inc.

Introduction

NEW FOR OLD?

In David Lodge's *Small World* (1984) Philip Swallow, an old-fashioned academic, gives a paper at an international conference which neatly sums up what might be called the 'Old Criticism':

> Philip Swallow was the first to speak. He said the function of criticism was to assist in the function of literature itself, which Dr Johnson had famously defined as enabling us better to enjoy life, or better to endure it. The great writers were men and women of exceptional wisdom, insight, and understanding. Their novels, plays and poems were inexhaustible reservoirs of values, ideas, images, which, when properly understood and appreciated, allowed us to live more fully, more finely, more intensely. But literary conventions changed, history changed, language changed, and these treasures too easily became locked away in libraries, covered with dust, neglected and forgotten. It was the job of the critic to . . . bring out the treasures into the light of day. Of course, he needed certain specialist skills to do this: a knowledge of history, a knowledge of philology, of generic convention and textual editing. But above all he needed enthusiasm, the love of books. It was by the demonstration of this enthusiasm in action that the critic forged a bridge between the great writers and the general reader. (*Small World*, Penguin, Harmondsworth, 1985, p. 317)

The so-called New Criticism, which prevailed between about 1930 and 1960, was partly an attempt to displace the amateurish impressionism celebrated by Swallow. The passage captures nicely the combination of moral and scholarly elements which make up the traditional virtues of English literary criticism. On the one hand, it is concerned with the celebration, preservation and communication of those 'universal human values' which remain unchallenged despite every change and revolution in human societies. On the other hand, the hand-maiden role of criticism requires it to expend much perspiration establishing

accurate texts, studying the development of the language, and discovering precise connections between texts and their 'background'. A
typically British 'common-sense' empiricism labours to preserve great
texts so that they can continue to transmit their eternal wisdom and to
yield emotional nourishment. Matthew Arnold, in the nineteenth
century, proclaimed that literature was a substitute for religion, astutely
grasping the fact that literature was able to satisfy an emotional need
created by the materialism of industrial society and modern science, a
need to which religion was responding less and less effectively. The
scholar's fastidious concern for factual accuracy is in the service of a
cultural mission to save humanity by preserving for it the great Sacred
Texts of Imaginative Literature. It must be said that the important
skills of textual and historical scholarship (vital to the editing of a text)
do not always serve such ideologically conservative purposes.

I have emphasised the split in the psyche of traditional literary
studies, because the division has such historical resonance. Until the
1960s modern criticism had its roots in the Romantic movement of the
late eighteenth and early nineteenth centuries. The Romantic poets
and critics offered people an 'imaginative' and 'creative' world of poetry
as a protest against and compensation for the harsh social and
economic realities of the industrial revolution. Utilitarianism in
political and economic philosophy and positivism in science seemed to
dominate life and reduce its humanity to a narrow round of calculation
and analysis. Gradgrind's utilitarian philosophy of 'fact' (in *Hard
Times*) wrings from Dickens a countervailing cry from the heart. The
Romantic rebellion took many forms. One strand worked to preserve
the separateness of literature and to elevate it to a cult object (Art for
Art's Sake). Another saw literature as providing a consolation and
focus for human feelings. The doctrine that literature is a substitute for
religion, providing a social cement and a balm for all social wounds and
class conflict, was a powerful Romantic legacy which nourished the
critical movements associated with the 'Rise of English'. The other side
of Philip Swallow's manifesto comes from the Germanic tradition in
classical scholarship which shaped earlier English studies. However,
New Criticism tried to establish a thoroughly professional discipline of
literary study which saw scholarship as the hand-maiden of criticism
and not the other way round. Even now the imaginary divide between
'critics' and 'scholars' can arouse mutual suspicion and hostility. The
scholar accuses the new-fangled critic of lacking a real discipline of
study, while the critic sneers at the 'dry-as-dust' and 'unimaginative'
work of the scholar.

NEW CRITICISM

The New Critics were the first group in Britain and the United States to claim that literary criticism could be a completely self-sufficient discipline, without relying upon an extra-literary apparatus of linguistic and historical skills, and that this could be achieved by concentrating on the close study of literary texts. Modern habits and methods of reading were successfully revolutionised by the New Critics, especially in the United States. In Britain, the demand for 'close reading' was first promoted by I. A. Richards in the 1920s, especially in his *Practical Criticism* (1929). 'Practical criticism' was later recuperated in a traditionally English form by F. R. and Q. D. Leavis, who focused on English literature as the treasure-house of civilised values. For the Leavisite critic (see also section 1) the quality of a text's form, imagery and style was inseparably bound up with the quality of its moral insights. The New Critics took over the Romantic concern for literature's imaginative unity and wholeness, but they infused this with a 'scientific' spirit of analysis. Each major work of literature was seen as a 'verbal icon', possessing an objectively achieved unity. A great poet creates an aesthetic structure which crystalises a complex response to human experience, a response which could not be expressed in other (non-literary) terms. Literary language was regarded as a special form of language which uses specific literary devices (paradox, irony, tension, ambiguity) in order to achieve a 'concrete' image of an otherwise inexpressible experience. The New Criticism, while appearing to be anti-Romantic in its professionalism and empiricism, was in fact a post-Romantic phenomenon. The separation of art as an autonomous practice has its roots in Romanticism (especially in Kantian aesthetics). Keats, for example, often treats poetry as a distinct and privileged form of thought. The New Critics addressed their 'objective' gaze at the poem not the poet, but managed to preserve the special sensibility of the poet in the form of the poem's unique linguistic form. It remained for the modern theories of structuralism, Marxism, feminism and poststructuralism to effect a true break with the Romantic inheritance.

MODERN THEORIES

I have dwelt upon the evolution of earlier modern literary criticism since the Romantics because recent developments in theory work against the tendencies I have described. Most contemporary theories are anti-Romantic, anti-humanistic, and anti-empiricist. They reject the privileging of emotion, the belief in the unity and identity of human subjectivity, and the blind faith in observation and experience as the only sources of knowledge. The main purpose of this book is to introduce these radical forms of theory and some of their antecedents, and to show their effects on reading practices. To put it simply, we can and must learn to *read differently*.

The recent outburst of criticial theory has not been welcomed by everyone. Some adopt a reactionary and philistine response to the challenge of new ideas, and resist anything of continental origin especially if it questions long-standing prejudices of British cultural institutions (this chauvinistic outlook is much less prevalent in the United States). Others are less defensive, and are genuinely engaged in trying to solve the problem of how to assimilate and make use of theories which are both difficult to understand and apparently remote from the spontaneous activity of reading. The difficulties encountered by the second type of reader are the ones this book aims to solve. It must be admitted that they are sometimes made worse by the uncompromising attitude of theorists, who are too often talking to one another in what looks like a private language of forbidding abstractness. First, I would say that conceptual difficulty cannot always be avoided. There is a real distinction to be made between jargon (or cant) and necessary concepts. The first can be translated into simpler terms, the second cannot without oversimplification. Structuralist terms such as 'signifier', 'signified', 'difference', 'binary opposition', and formalist terms such as 'defamiliarisation' and 'device' are not only necessary to their critical discourses but also intrinsically no more difficult than other concepts which we have become used to (imagination, creativity, organic unity, irony, tension, and so on). New ideas require new concepts.

After Philip Swallow's conference speech on the old criticism the next speakers proclaim the virtues of post-New Critical theories (no one represents the now unfashionable middle ground of New Criticism). David Lodge neatly summarises the new theories and at the same time satirises them. He also brings out the competition between theories. Michel Tardieu (the French seem to be fond of christening their structuralist-inclined offspring 'Michel'; and there is a French theorist called 'Bordieu') announces that criticism is no longer interested in interpreting individual works but in uncovering the 'fun-

damental laws which enable such works to be produced and understood'. Structuralism aspires to the knowledge of the 'deep structural
principles and binary oppositions that underlay all texts that had ever
been written and that ever would be written: paradigm and syntagm,
metaphor and metonymy, mimesis and diegesis (*Small World*, p. 318).

Siegfried von Turpitz, in support of reader-response theories, rejects
attempts to define literary texts in terms of their formal properties,
since they 'enjoyed only an as it were virtual existence until they were
realised in the mind of the reader'. Fulvia Morgana presents the
neo-Marxist view: criticism's function is to:

> wage undying war on the very concept of 'literature' itself, which was
> nothing more than an instrument of bourgeois hegemony, a fetishistic
> reification of so-called aesthetic values erected and maintained through an
> élitist educational system in order to conceal the brutal facts of class
> oppression under industrial capitalism. (*Small World*, p. 318)

The French structuralist, the German 'reception' theorist and the
Italian Marxist each reject the older critical values but also each
other's.

It is true that the ideological wrangling among exponents of different
theories will be disheartening and off-putting to the uninitiated.
However, contemporary theories are not as sectarian as Lodge's satire
suggests; each major current has opened itself to the range of movements. For example, feminist, Marxist and psychoanalytic criticisms
have all undergone marked deconstructive inflections, following their
individual encounters with Derrida. Critical theories are not like
tablets of stone, unaffected by the passage of time. Marxist thought, for
example, has continued to sharpen and renew the insights of the
founding fathers in the light of new knowledge. Influential revisions of
Marxist and Freudian theories draw upon structuralist linguistics.

Students will want to know which tradition has the best claim to
truth, validity, relevance, or explanatory power. I do not claim to be
neutral on this question, because in the end no theory can totally
transcend its ideological prehistory. My own critical orientation cannot
and should not be suppressed in an effort to guarantee the validity of
this book's map of the critical field. I regard the dislodging of both 'Old'
and 'New' criticisms from dominant positions as a positive and
progressive development in several respects. Traditional 'scholarship',
New Criticism and the Scrutiny movement were all founded upon
backward-looking ideologies. Leavis and the New Critics retreated into
a nostalgia for pre-capitalist, 'organic' societies (which were essentially

imaginary); the Old Criticism often complied with imperialist and Romantic views of culture; 'scholarship', beating a retreat from overt ideology, embraced a reactionary 'positivist' (pseudo-scientific) relationship to texts, and denied their social and historical engagements. As these remarks imply, I have written this book from a perspective sympathetic to a 'materialist' position, open to Marxist, feminist and poststructuralist currents, all of which seek to engage in a major critique of human culture. These theories share a commitment to unravelling the entire project of Western 'bourgeois' humanism and to questioning notions such as the autonomy of the individual, the unity and stability of the 'normal' self and the universality of essential human valves. This powerful series of discourses raises fundamental questions about:

1. Identity and subjectivity.
2. The nature of representation.
3. The processes of history.

The theories discussed in this book all touch upon these issues in some way.

Having mastered the range of concepts provided by critical theories, how can we learn to use them? In a sense this is a falsely posed question, because theory and practice should not be so awkwardly divorced. Two reasons for resistance to the study of theory are the theorist's habit of treating theories as independent of practice, and the practitioner's blindness to the presence of theory in every practice. It is more sensible to grasp a theory and its potential value by observing it at work. However, I have decided that students need a brief introduction to concepts before seeing them put to work. *Practising Theory* tries to show how contemporary theories can develop and extend the practice of reading, and is conceived as a counterpart to my earlier *A Reader's Guide to Contemporary Literary Theory* (1985). I wrote the first book because I thought that the field could be introduced clearly and simply without destroying its serious significance. Subsequently, teachers have suggested to me that I should provide a complementary study addressed more directly to *practice*. I have not assumed that the *Reader's Guide* is always at hand, and have therefore included brief glances at the theories before launching into specific readings. Readers will find that the two books have a similar structure. I would not wish readers to accept such thin theoretical presentations as adequate preparation. They should continue to explore theories at the same time as working with them in practice. Without this commitment to *theoretical practice* the subsequent critical practice will be bloodless and routine. There is such a thing as theoretical subtlety, and critics should not be ashamed of their desire to refine theory as long as it is done in the spirit of *praxis*. This Marxist term has several implications. First, theoretical work must always address itself to the 'real world', and not take flight into a stratospheric region beyond actual human societies. Secondly, theories will, in any case, always possess some social and political interest or commitment. I will sometimes point out the ideological freight carried by each theory, to avoid giving the impression that all theories carry the same ideological burden or even that they have managed somehow to shed their load like Bunyan's Christian approaching the Celestial City.

WHICH THEORY?

People who write introductory studies like to create an impression that their fields of study are neatly unified. It would be nice to be able to present a systematic and easily digested exposition of theories and their applications running smoothly from chapter to chapter. However, although the long established 'hegemony' of Leavis and the New Critics is over, no single monolithic critical tradition has taken its place. The old hegemony has been challenged by structuralist, psychoanalytic, neo-Marxist, deconstructive, neo-formalist, reader-response and feminist critical schools (to name only the most prominent). None of these interventions individually has been decisive in re-shaping critical practice, but taken together they have radically shifted the focus of literary criticism.

Given a situation of *de facto* pluralism, it makes sense to offer an introduction to the theory and practice of modern criticism which explores this multiplicity. The danger of my format is that it may appear to convey a judicious but deceitful neutrality. I have tried to retain a certain critical curiosity and openness towards the current cosmopolitan atmosphere, but I have not suppressed my own evaluation of particular approaches. It may seem best to say 'let many flowers bloom' and to treat the plenitude of theories as a cornucopia to be enjoyed and tasted with relish. However, I am not a salesman or broker and I reject a 'market economy' attitude towards critical theory.

Certain theories are less subversive than others, and have been more or less successfully adapted to conventional methods of reading. For example, deconstruction and the philosophy of Derrida have won many hearts and minds in the United States mainly because it was so easy to translate the methods and concepts of New Criticism into this new and exciting critical discourse. Deconstruction has been a less seductive suitor in Britain, where New Criticism never became an orthodoxy as it did in the States, but Christopher Norris's Fontana Masters study of Derrida (1988) points the way towards a more 'political' and even 'objective' form of deconstruction. I have been impressed by the way in which some Marxist and feminist critics have pillaged and cannibalised the concepts of formalism, structuralism, psychoanalysis and deconstruction without negating their political and social commitments. Some have criticised Terry Eagleton and Fredric Jameson for indulging in trendy and opportunistic forays into continental theories at the expense of political purity. However, it must be said that no historical form of thought has ever outlived its first maturity without engaging with the changing historical reality and enlarging its scope by judicious assimilation of fresh conceptual food.

At this point I would like to foreground the variety of theories by attempting four brief readings of a passage from William Blake's *America*. The poem is an allegorical vision of the rebellion of the American colonies under George III which led to the American War of Independence. The reactionary English government ('Albion's Angel') sees revolution rising across the Atlantic:

> Albion's Angel stood beside the Stone of night, and saw
> The terror like a comet, or more like the planet red
> That once enclos'd the terrible wandering comets in its sphere.
> Then, Mars, thou wast our center, & the planets three flew round
> Thy crimson disk: so e'er the Sun was rent from thy red sphere.
> The Spectre glow'd his horrid length staining the temple long
> With beams of blood; & thus a voice came forth, and shook the temple:
> 'The morning comes, the night decays, the watchmen leave their
>   stations;
> 'The grave is burst, the spices shed, the linen wrapped up;
> 'The bones of death, the cov'ring clay, the sinews shrunk & dry'd
> 'Reviving shake, inspiring move, breathing, awakening,
> 'Spring like redeemed captives when their bonds & bars are burst.
> 'Let the slave grinding at the mill run out into the field,
> 'Let him look up into the heavens & laugh in the bright air;
> 'Let the inchained soul, shut up in darkness and in sighing,
> 'Whose face has never seen a smile in thirty weary years,
> 'Rise and look out; his chains are loose, his dungeon doors are open;

'And let his wife and children return from the oppressor's scourge.
'They look behind them at every step & believe it is a dream,
'Singing: "The sun has left his blackness & has found a fresher morning,
'"And the fair Moon rejoices in the clear & cloudless night;
'"For Empire is no more, and now the Lion & Wolf shall cease."'
(from *America, Poetry and Prose*, ed. Geoffrey Keynes (Nonesuch Press,
London, 1961, pp. 202–3))

A Formalist Approach

I include under this heading both American and Russian types of
formalism. For a formalist it is the 'literariness' of Blake's language
which demands attention. Its fusion of a Miltonic style of epic grandeur
and a Biblical style of ritual simplicity asks for detailed analysis from a
formalist viewpoint. The use of epic simile ('like a comet') is
reminiscent of Milton. The Biblical element is present in the short
clauses linked by parataxis ('The grave is burst, the spices shed, the
linen wrapped up'), and in the repeated (anaphoric) structures ('Let . . .
Let . . . Let'; 'his chains . . . his dungeon doors . . . his wife'). A New
Critic would dwell upon the *tension* between two sets of connotations
associated with the 'Spectre' (of Revolution): it resembles the warlike
planet of Mars in appearance, but speaks of clear skies, of resurrection
and of the end of oppression and war. The tension between imagery of
war and of peace is to be understood poetically: the desire to end
oppression and empire is a *threat* to Albion's Angel whose harsh and
hypocritical rule depends upon American willingness to be exploited.
The Spectre *looks* warlike to the bitter Angel, despite the talk of peace.
Formalists look for:

1. The deformation of ordinary language.
2. The poetic devices which 'defamiliarise' automatised conventions
   or perceptions.
3. The tensions, ambiguities, or paradoxes, with which the poet
   grasps the complexity of experience.

The strictly formalist view is 'scientific' in spirit, refusing to open out
theory to grasp the articulations of artistic form with other systems of
meaning. The New Critics were, in this respect, less purist: they
wanted to preserve a link between the poet's technique and his or her
apprehension of 'experience'. Blake's technique in this case is valued in
so far as it embodies successfully a rich sense of life's tensions and
contradictions.

A Marxist Approach

Marxist critics usually refuse to treat 'literature' as a privileged category of discourse, even though they acknowledge its special significance for any study of ideology. From a Marxist viewpoint Blake's poem is both a subversive text and a text which contains (controls and limits) its subversiveness. Its 'dialectical' insights succeed in undermining the single vision of imperialist ideology. Blake uses the terms 'Angel' and 'Stone' in negative senses: the 'virtuous' and complacent morality of imperialism is built upon a perverted righteousness. The mosaic 'Stone' is transformed from the tablet of the Lord to an oppressive Law. Later the Spectre declares: 'That stony law I stamp to dust.' The voice of revolution speaks of oppression in images of imprisonment and forced labour ('the slave grinding at the mill', 'the inchained soul'). Blake thus gives a voice to the oppressed masses who yearn for the end of Empire. However, by encapsulating his 'vision' in mythic form, Blake, from a Marxist viewpoint, has assured the self-containment of his subversive questioning of ruling-class ideology. The dialectical patterns of the poem capture brilliantly the *processes of history*, but at the same time history is drained of concreteness and specificity by a relentless abstractness and allegorical retreat from actuality. A more historically focused Marxist critic might argue that Blake's radicalism was inevitably marginalised and rarefied at a time (1793) when the repressive apparatus of the state was at its strongest.

A Reader-response Approach

There are several types of reader-response criticism, but most of them would begin by asking questions about the reader's experience in the act of reading the text. Readers must begin by grasping the poem's genre. Only by reading it as allegorical epic can we understand the basic narrative discourse about angels, spectres, temple-shaking cosmic voices and so on. If we treat the passage as the beginning of the poem, we can say that our first response to the opening lines is going to be corrected by what follows (unless we are already familiar with Blake's poetic methods). 'Angel' has positive connotations, 'terror' negative connotations. The next sentence faces the reader with a statement which flies in the face of conventional astronomy: 'Mars, thou wast our center'. One way of 'naturalising' this statement is to take it as the author's private 'myth'. Other reader-response critics would be interested in studying the reception of Blake's poetry in his time and later. It is clear that this would produce a fascinating result: Blake was known and admired by a very small circle, and only gradually after W. B. Yeats's famous edition did he become regarded as a major Romantic poet, and finally in the late 1960s became a cult figure for the 'Beat' generation. This type of reception theory, because it takes historical change into account, is more compatible with a Marxist view of the passage.

A *Structuralist Approach*

A structuralist might concentrate on the figurative level of the poem's discourse. Roman Jakobson shows that linguistic structures may be used as keys to open literary structures. 'Binary oppositions', for example, enable us to define individual features in a discourse as significant. The opposition between 'metaphor' and 'metonymy' reflects a central binary aspect of language – the paradigmatic (vertical) and syntagmatic (horizontal) dimensions. Metaphor works by selecting parallels from paradigmatic sets and systems, while metonymy works by focusing upon individual elements in the syntagmatic sequence. Metaphor departs from context, metonymy adheres to context. Metaphor, says Jacobson, is typical of Romantic and Symbolist poetry, while metonomy is typical of realistic fiction. In the Blake passage, as we would expect, metaphor predominates: every element which might represent a specific context actually opens the way continually to other contexts. For example, 'the inchained soul' can be an actual prisoner, or any oppressed person (in metaphoric chains). The openness is apparent in the unusual combination of material and spiritual terms: the 'soul' stands for 'man', who has a 'face' and a 'wife and children'. Albion's Angel stands beside a stone, which we understand to refer to the English government and to its laws. I believe that this type of structural analysis, while it is strictly ahistorical (metaphor and metonymy are universal figures), can be given a historical 'turn'. It is a valuable piece of conceptual equipment for a critic who aims to define particular historical literary forms. The germ of this value is present in Roman Jakobson's perception that particular artistic forms lean towards one or other figure (Romantic poetry to metaphor, realistic prose to metonymy).

These are just four possible approaches to the passage. The exercises at the end of the book will enable readers to attempt different readings. Why should we try to think ourselves into such disparate theoretical frames of reference? Should we try to synthesise them? Should we try to be eclectic and accommodate the best insights into a single comprehensive reading? Should we choose the 'best' theory? In my view, we can hardly avoid making choices, especially since every theory has profound implications for political, moral and metaphysical commitments. We will probably wish to adopt or adapt approaches which seem to raise central and urgent questions. My four readings of the Blake extract are accented in certain ways to bring out their possible value for a materialist or historical form of criticism. Readers must decide which questions are likely to direct the current of their life energies into congenial channels. This does not mean that nothing can be gained from a comprehensive understanding of the whole field. After all, many of the best critics ingeniously combine a wide range of concepts in their chosen theoretical discourses.

The influx of continental Marxist and structuralist writings, the translation of Russian Formalist texts and the rise of feminist theories together signalled the beginning of a decisive shift in the teaching and practice of criticism. The structuralist 'moment' was rapidly superseded by the poststructuralist interventions of Derrida, Lacan, Foucault and Barthes. Marxist and feminist critics have negotiated these transitions with considerable inventiveness. We are still working through the legacy of the late 1960s.

This book presents the new theories at work in a sequence of readings which follows more or less the ordering of the theories discussed in my *Reader's Guide to Contemporary Literary Theory* (1985, 2nd edn 1989). Starting with a few examples of critical methods which were dominant in the 1940s and 1950s, I pass through the most influential tendencies: formalism, structuralism, poststructuralism, reader-response theories, feminism and Marxism. The final chapter offers exercises for discussion in seminars. I have raised a number of questions which may be explored by teachers and students. It would be possible to substitute different literary examples. I would expect discussions to focus on the question of the value and scope of particular theories in providing the answers to those questions which seem worth asking. I myself do not wish to recommend the adoption of every theory discussed in the book. The Russian Formalist concepts, for example, are, in my view, of value only when located within a body of theory which articulates the various levels and types of discourse within a social formation as a whole. Nevertheless, the full range of theories must be understood by anyone who aims to chart a meaningful route through modern criticism. The exercises should help the reader to grasp the differences between the questions raised and answers given by the various theories. Teachers will no doubt wish to assist students to see the ways in which it would be possible to prioritise the questions one might ask about literary texts. For example, reader-response theories may provide useful concepts and methods to assist a materialist study of literature and ideology. After all, for ideology to work at the textual level it must be able to achieve the acquiescence of the reader. In this instance, questions about the reader's response are subordinated to those about ideology.

I have written two short introductory books about literary theory mainly because I believe that all literary students now need to take on board the intellectual challenge of modern theories. The terms and values which underpinned the critical writings of Leavis, T. S. Eliot, Cleanth Brooks and I. A. Richards lost their currency long ago. This book is a modest attempt to help readers to begin mastering new positions and new concepts for the study of literary texts. The theories take us some way into philosophy, politics, linguistics and psychology without leaving the ground of literary criticism. Students of literature can now develop skills which will enable them to demystify the basic coordinates of literary communication. Concepts such as 'author', 'work', 'representation', 'expression' and 'intention' were once part of a seamlessly unified language of criticism which resisted theoretical scrutiny. New concepts such as 'sign', 'subject', 'difference', 'discourse', 'enunciation' and 'textuality' not only disrupt the older ones but form part of properly articulated theories. This book invites readers to make the transition from an untheoretised set of mainly post-Romantic assumptions to a mainly poststructuralist (or even postmodern) set. The latter positions remain as *positions* but can liberate readers from hidebound and unexamined critical conventions. My own commitment is to a materialist and historical form of theory which draws upon the new concepts for support. However, the book is not strictly governed by this agenda, and can facilitate the development of other critical strategies.

INTRODUCTORY READING

The following are some useful introductory books in the field of literary theory:
Belsey, Catherine, *Critical Practice* (Methuen, London, 1980).

14 Practising Theory and Reading Literature

Culler, Jonathan, *Structuralist Poetics* (Routledge & Kegan Paul, London, 1975).

Davis, Robert Con, ed., *Contemporary Literary Criticism: Modernism through Poststructuralism* (Longman, London and New York, 1986). Good, but difficult psychoanalysis selection.

Eagleton, Terry, *Marxism and Literary Criticism* (Methuen, London and New York, 1976).

Eagleton, Terry, *Literary Theory: An Introduction* (Blackwell, Oxford, 1984). Exhilarating.

Ellmann, Mary, *Thinking about Women* (Macmillan, London, 1968; Virago Press, London, 1979).

Erlich, Victor, *Russian Formalism: History – Doctrine* (3rd edn, Yale University Press, New Haven and London, 1981).

Fokkema, D. W. and E. Kunne-Ibsch, eds, *The Theories of Literature in the Twentieth Century: Structuralism, Marxism, Aesthetics of Reception, Semiotics* (C. Hurst, London, 1977).

Frow, John, *Marxism and Literary History* (Blackwell, Oxford, 1986).

Hawkes, Terence, *Structuralism and Semiotics* (Methuen, London, 1977).

Holub, Robert C., *Reception Theory: A Critical Introduction* (Methuen, London and New York, 1984).

Jameson, Fredric, *The Prison-House of Language: A Critical Account of Structuralism and Russian Formalism* (Princeton University Press, Princeton and London, 1972).

Jefferson, Ann and David Robey, eds, *Literary Theory, A Comparative Introduction* (Batsford, London, 2nd edn, 1986). Good reading lists.

Lambropoulos, V. and D. N. Miller, eds, *20th-Century Literary Theory: An Introductory Anthology* (State University of New York Press, Albany, NY, 1987). Concentrates on New Criticism and Russian (and Czech) Formalism.

Lentricchia, Frank, *After the New Criticism* (Athlone Press, London, 1980).

Lodge, David, ed., *20th-Century Literary Criticism* (Longman, London, 1972).

Lodge, David, *The Modes of Modern Writing: Metaphor, Metonymy, and the Typology of Modern Literature* (Arnold, London, 1977).

Lodge, David, ed., *Modern Criticism and Theory* (Longman, London and New York, 1988). Authoritative reader (post-1960 theories) except on structuralist and Marxist criticism.

Machin, Richard and Christopher Norris, eds, *Post-structuralist Read-*

ings of English Poetry (Cambridge University Press, Cambridge, London and New York, 1987).

Moi, Toril, *Sexual/Textual Politics: Feminist Literary Theory* (Methuen, London and New York, 1985).

Newton, K. M., *Twentieth-Century Literary Theory: A Reader* (Macmillan, Basingstoke and London, 1988).

Norris, Christopher, *Deconstruction: Theory and Practice* (Methuen, London, 1982). Lucid.

Rice, Philip and Patricia Waugh, eds, *Modern Literary Theory: A Reader* (Arnold, London, New York, Melbourne, Auckland, 1989).

Ruthven, K. K., *Feminist Literary Studies* (Cambridge University Press, Cambridge, London and New York, 1984).

Rylance, Rick, ed., *Debating Texts: A Reader in 20th-Century Literary Theory and Method* (Open University Press, Milton Keynes, 1987). Good, but weak on reader-response and Marxist critics.

Selden, Raman, *A Reader's Guide to Contemporary Literary Theory* (Harvester Press, Brighton, 1985; 2nd edn, 1989).

Selden, Raman, ed., *The Theory of Criticism from Plato to the Present* (Longman, London and New York, 1988). Places contemporary theories in the context of critical history.

Showalter, Elaine, ed., *The New Feminist Criticism* (Pantheon Books, New York, 1985; Virago Press, London, 1986).

Suleiman, Susan and Inge Crosman, eds, *The Reader in the Text: Essays on Audience and Interpretation* (Princeton University Press, Princeton, NJ, 1980).

Tallack, Douglas, ed., *Literary Theory at Work: 3 Texts* (Batsford, London, 1987). Useful. Good reading lists.

Tomkins, Jane P., ed., *Reader-Response Criticism: From Formalism to Post-Structuralism* (Johns Hopkins University Press, 1980).

Todorov, Tzvetan, *Introduction to Poetics*, trans. R. Howard (Harvester Press, Brighton, 1981).

Williams, Raymond, *Marxism and Literature* (Oxford University Press, Oxford, 1977).

Wright, Elizabeth, *Psychoanalytic Criticism: Theory in Practice* (Methuen, London and New York, 1984).

Young, Robert, ed., *Untying the Text* (Routledge & Kegan Paul, Boston, London and Henley, 1981). Useful poststructuralist anthology.

Chapter 1

Anglo-American Criticism

Section 1

Text: John Bunyan, *Pilgrim's Progress*
Theory: Moral Criticism (F. R. Leavis)

Many of the major figures in the history of British literary criticism have been in some sense 'moral' critics. They include Sir Philip Sidney, Samuel Johnson, Percy Shelley, Matthew Arnold and F. R. Leavis. For this reason, Leavis has the appearance of an 'organic intellectual', whose roots are firmly secured in native soil. However, in his day he was regarded by many as a rancorous dogmatist. In particular, he offended what we might call the literary 'establishment', which, in his view, was amateurish, genteel and completely unable to recognise the fundamental importance of literature in the struggle to preserve humane values in a world dominated by cheap commercialism. *Scrutiny* (1932–53) was the journal established by Leavis at Cambridge to carry the banner of civilised values, which he identified with the values of the 'Great Tradition' in English writing.

Moral criticism in its modern forms is the most 'natural' of critical practices and the least theoretically self-conscious or explicit. Indeed its concepts and its values must be 'felt' as connected with human 'experience' and not treated as abstractions or provisional theories. Intuitively their validity must appear to be self-evident if they are to remain in force. While Marxists and feminists base their approach on theories of oppression and domination, moral criticism draws upon the terms of general moral discourse: 'maturity', 'seriousness', 'wholeness', 'authenticity' 'sincerity', 'life', 'sanity'. Because the words have a universal import, they appear timeless and unquestionable. However, if we examine the practice of moral critics, we find that they are not in accord with one another in their judgements. Matthew Arnold's use of the term 'serious' is different from Leavis's use. The latter admired Arnold, but felt that the key Arnoldian term, 'high seriousness', was an 'insistent nuisance'. Leavis resisted the classical and aristocratic bearing of Arnold's terminology, and preferred the term 'profound seriousness' because it did not suggest Victorian dignity or classical stateliness. For Leavis, seriousness was deeply rooted in English non-conformist culture, while for Arnold puritanism with its Hebraic 'strictness of conscience' always required a culture of Hellenic 'sweetness and light' to give it humanity.

This illustration is intended to show that moral criticisms rest upon what appear to be foundations of untouchable and intuitive values, which are in turn grounded in social commitments. The strength of this type of critical position is that its assumptions are secured at a very deep level and are not usually open to question. Those who share a particular complex constellation of values and underpinning social identifications do not need to examine them or justify them to those who uncomprehendingly reject them. Leavis characteristically appeals to his readers by assuming that they are responding sensitively and unerringly to his delicate observations of a text's inner meaning and profundity. He writes of the 'felt life', the 'humanity', or the 'maturity' of a particular text as being *there* on the page as if it were a physical property. It is not possible to adopt Leavis's 'method' except at an intuitive level. We can learn to be a moral critic only by imbibing an entire attitude and set of values without inspecting them with detachment or exploring their theoretical implications. If it were possible to render such moral criticism explicit as a set of theories, the result would be disastrous: what should be intuitive and 'felt' would become intellectualised and abstract. In this respect it differs from merely moralistic criticism which imposes an explicit theory of moral rules or behaviour.

This insistence on the 'concreteness' of critical practice is fundamental to Leavis's work and corresponds to his view of literature itself. He believed that the best literary texts were not reducible to abstract summary or to generalised statement. The tragic aspect of a Shakespearean play cannot be expressed as an idea or as a philosophical statement; the tragic quality is something inseparable from the poetic language of the play – it is 'enacted' in poetry. Keats's 'Ode to a Nightingale' possesses an 'extraordinary intensity of realisation' and also an 'extraordinary rightness and delicacy of touch'. We cannot wrench a meaning or statement from the poem without destroying this specificity of enactment, this concreteness of realisation. It is often difficult for the non-initiated reader to grasp the nuances of Leavis's argument. This is because his concepts must remain unexamined: the judgements involve the activity of a 'sensibility' which operates intuitively. In this respect Leavis's intuitive form of empiricism differs from American New Criticism's method. The New Critics were committed on an 'objective' form of textual analysis which did not rely upon assertions of sensibility for its evidence. In an essay on Bunyan, Leavis chooses to discuss the following passage in which Christian talks to the self-seeking, worldly and time-serving By-ends:

> Christian. Pray, who are your kindred . . .? if a man may be so bold.
> By-ends. Almost the whole town; and in particular, my Lord *Turn-about*, my Lord *Time-server*, my Lord *Fair-speech* . . . also Mr *Smooth-man*, Mr *Facing-both-ways*, Mr *Any-thing*; and the parson of our parish, Mr *Two-tongues*, was my mother's own brother by father's side; and to tell you the truth, I am become a gentleman of good quality, yet my great-grandfather was but a waterman, looking one way and rowing another, and I got most of my estate by the same occupation.
> Christian. Are you a married man?
> By-ends. Yes, my wife is a very virtuous woman, the daughter of a virtuous woman; she was my Lady *Feigning*'s daughter, there-fore she came of a very honourable family, and is arrived to such a pitch of breeding, that she knows how to carry it to all, even to prince and peasant. It is true we somewhat differ in religion from those of the stricter sort, yet but in two small points: first, we never strive against wind and tide; secondly, we are always most zealous when religion goes in his silver slippers; we love much to walk with him in the street, if the sun shines, and the people applaud him.
> (from John Bunyan, *The Pilgrim's Progress* (Folio Society, London 1962, pp. 94–5))

Leavis comments:

> This is plainly traditional art and, equally plainly the life in it is of the people. . . . The names and racy turns are organic with the general style, and the style, concentrating the life of popular idiom, is the expression of popular habit – the expression of a vigorous humane culture. For what is involved is not merely an idiomatic raciness of speech, expressing a strong vitality, but an art of social living, with its mature habits of valuation. (*The Common Pursuit*, p. 208)

Note how Leavis weaves together strands of stylistic commentary and cultural evaluation. The 'popular idiom' is the 'expression of popular habit'; what is involved is 'an *art* of *social living*'. In this he follows Arnold's critical practice, refusing to separate the aesthetic from the moral: excellence of style is always also excellence of values. Bunyan's popular idiom is an *expression* of a particular civilisation. Leavis does not justify this evaluation; it is simply asserted as a matter of tacit agreement between him and the reader. Any reader who simply cannot accept the judgement would be deemed to lack the necessary fineness of judgement.

Earlier he talks of the book's 'rich, poised and mature humanity'. He adds significantly:

> And this is not the less impressive for our being, here and there, by the allegorical intent of this or that incident, reminded of the uglier and pettier aspects of the intolerant creed, the narrow scheme of personal salvation, that Bunyan explicitly sets out to allegorize. (p. 206).

Here Leavis faces head-on the strongest reason for disliking Bunyan's classic. Bunyan was a nonconformist preacher in a period of heroic endurance under Charles II. The Calvinist theology which his anabaptist church espoused seems rather forbidding to many modern readers. Calvin believed in man's utter depravity and in God's infinite goodness. This desperate contrast led him to assert the terrible doctrine of 'predestination', according to which God, at the beginning of time, 'elected' certain individuals to be saved. This generosity of God was totally undeserved; nothing a human being can do by way of good works can merit the grace which God freely gives to some. Most Puritans who followed these beliefs were motivated to devote themselves to a good life, despite the unworthiness of all human endeavours, in the belief that in so doing they might find assurance of God's grace. Leavis's remarks touch rather tangentially upon all this, but his essential point is clear: the morally repugnant side of Calvinism is completely transcended in Bunyan's great work. *Pilgrim's Progress* is not a piece of applied theology but the embodiment of a whole way of life. Many important English writers and much of English socialist thought is deeply coloured by this Puritan 'civilisation'.

The passage on By-ends includes a deep strain of Puritan ideology: the worldliness and compromising spirit of the Church of England is evidently in Bunyan's sights. Social snobbery, gentility, time-serving – these are all targets of Bunyan's Puritan satire, which contrasts with and is a reply to the long tradition of neo-classical anti-Puritan satire running from Ben Jonson (Tribulation Wholesome in *The Alchemist*, and Zeal-of-the-Land Busy in *Bartholomew Fair* are famous examples) to Samuel ('Hudibras') Butler and John Dryden, Bunyan's contemporaries. Leavis's profound admiration for Bunyan is not openly ideological. He does not say, 'Yes, there Bunyan expresses that disdain for the unprincipled and shallow values of a ruling élite. He advances a Puritan culture of the common people which was shared by George

Eliot and D. H. Lawrence, whose work I admire for similar reasons.' In other words Leavis's 'moral' response to Bunyan necessarily conceals allegiances which cannot be directly presented to the reader. To support overtly the values embodied in Bunyan's writings would expose them to question and possible rejection on political grounds. Some Marxist and feminist critics are more honest about their commitments, and thereby open themselves to rejection on overtly ideological grounds.

Leavis's form of moral criticism is compatible with the traditions of practical criticism which developed under the aegis of the New Criticism during the 1930s. A writer's moral seriousness is always enacted in literary language and is never merely an expression of moral ideas. However, it is clear that Leavis *does* respond to a particular form of moral vision associated with a particular notion of English civilisation, which he finds in Bunyan but not, for example, in Laurence Sterne or Thomas Hardy. It is also clear that a quite different embodiment of English civilisation might be constructed, which was equally anti-establishment. Edward Bond, the radical dramatist, dismisses the Puritan tradition too when he enunciates the basis of *his* moral vision: 'The world is unhappy and violent not because we're cursed with original sin *or* original aggression, but because it is unjust. The world is not absurd, it is finally a place for men to be sane and rational in' (*Bingo*, 1974, p. xii). A moral criticism based upon this set of exclusions and assumptions would take a very different form from Leavis's. However, they have one thing in common: their unrelenting commitment to moral seriousness has offended their ideological enemies. Can major writers avoid giving offence? Can a critic's or a writer's moral vision be universal in its appeal? A great deal of modern critical writing suggests that moral vision is always ideological (that is, it is a historically-determined, 'imaginary' reflection of 'real' social relations).

Does this mean that once we see a moral perspective as ideological it ceases to have any validity? To be effective as critics must we be blind to our own ideological commitments? Marxist and feminist critics, it seems to me, have recognised the need to heal the breech between 'fact' and 'value'. They understand that literary criticism can never transcend human values and interests. On the other hand, they have had the courage of their convictions: they claim validity for their theories without disguising the commitments which underpin them. Leavis's moral criticism is concerned with selection, evaluation and exclusion, on grounds which are never purely 'literary' or totally disinterested. Moral criticism, it seems, cannot survive unless it believes it embraces everything that is worthwhile in human existence, and answers the reader's deepest needs for moral vision. Its weakness lies in its self-deceiving claim to disinterestedness and universality.

Section 2

Text: John Keats, 'Ode to a Nightingale'
Theory: New Criticism

As a young student of English I imbibed the language of New Criticism with very little awareness of its theoretical specificity. I used terms such as 'imagery', 'form', 'tone', 'paradox', 'irony', 'tension', 'ambiguity' and 'unity' with no awareness that they formed part of a more or less consistent theory. It was only later that I read essays by Cleanth Brooks, W. K. Wimsatt and Monroe Beardsley, which expressed New Critical positions in theoretical terms. However, it would be wrong to suppose that New Criticism tried to develop a completely articulated theory in the manner of Russian Formalism. The Romantic inheritance, which the New Critics sought to challenge, persisted as a source of incoherence in their own thinking. What remained unresolved and unresolvable in New Critical theorising was the relationship between two central assertions:

1. That poems possess organic unity and autonomy.
2. That poems give us rich and 'concrete' apprehensions of experience.

In their influential text book, *Understanding Poetry* (3rd edition, 1960; 1st edition, 1938), Cleanth Brooks and Robert Penn Warren discuss 'How Poems Come About'. Their account is an uneasy attempt to bring the two assertions into harmony. Wordsworth's daffodil poem is founded upon a specific experience (recorded in Dorothy Wordsworth's diary) but the process of composition is not simply a transcription of experience because the poem is built upon many types of material of which 'experience' is only one. Other poems, they point out, may have no direct links with experiences. T. S. Eliot, who was an important influence on the New Critics, believed that the best poems do not derive from personal experience and that the poet's mind is a sort of 'impersonal' laboratory in which materials of many sorts (literary, philosophical, experiential) are given new forms. We judge a poem not as a record of experience but as an achieved 'verbal icon'. Brooks and Warren emphasise that the meaning of a poem cannot be reduced to anything outside the poem, whether it is an experience, an idea, or an intention. Whatever the starting point may be, the poet proceeds in the manner of a craftsman. Here are a few sentences from their account:

> He may start with a personal experience as yet uninterpreted, a general vague feeling, an episode, a metaphor, a phrase – anything that comes along to excite the imagination. . . . At the same time that he is trying to envisage the poem as a whole, he is trying to relate the individual items to that whole. He cannot assemble them in a merely arbitrary fashion; they must bear some relation to each other. So he develops his sense of the whole, the anticipation of the finished poem, as he works with the parts, and moves from one part to another. Then, as the sense of the whole develops, it modifies the process by which the poet selects and relates the parts, the words, images, rhythms, local ideas, events, etc. . . . . It is an infinitely complicated process of establishing interrelations. (pp. 526–7)

This dialectic between parts and the whole emerges here as a technical problem rather than an experiential one. However, underlying the concern with technique is an ideological project which is never far from the surface in the work of the New Critics. A pessimistic and conservative assessment of modern society drives the critic to find in poetry what is not present in society; the poet's rage for order, the struggle to unify disparate experience, is a desperate act of faith in the face of a chaotic world in which all faith and meaning has gone. There is also a latent correspondence between this organicism and a certain kind of American social theory, which regards society as a conflict-free, smoothly functioning, mutually adjusting set of interrelations. It is evident, therefore, that the New Critics are not 'formalists' in the strict sense, because they refuse to acknowledge that their analytic approach is finally in the service of a humanistic and moral crusade. Great poets are great because their poems embody, in language which cannot be re-expressed in ordinary words, the contradictory and unresolvable tensions of experience. What is presupposed here is that great poets will reveal no absolute commitments, will make no unequivocal statements, and will allow no easy resolutions of conflicts and tensions. Great writers, in a word, will be moderates. The New Critics were fond of quoting Keats's celebrated definition of the poet's 'negative capability' – 'when a man is capable of being in uncertainties, mysteries, doubts, without any irritable reaching after fact and reason' (letter to G. & T. Keats, 21 December 1817). It is easy to persuade ourselves that all great writers will rise in this fashion above the mêlée of power struggles and ideological confrontations. However, we should not overlook the ideological bearings of this 'impersonality', nor forget that New Criticism's commitments have the effect of marginalising writers such as Milton, Bunyan, Blake and Brecht, whose negative capability is less evident than is the case with Shakespeare, Donne, Marvell and T. S. Eliot.

Keats's poem 'Ode to a Nightingale' responds admirably to the 'close reading' techniques of New Criticism. Essays by Cleanth Brooks, Earl Wasserman and F. R. Leavis (in some respects a New Critic) have demonstrated the complexity, ambiguity, and tension, sustained throughout the poem. There is no space here to explore the entire poem, but I shall concentrate on stanza six, in which the poet, at the height of his imaginative identification with the bird wishes for death. Here is the stanza:

> Darkling I listen; and for many a time
> I have been half in love with easeful Death,
> Called him soft names in many a mused rhyme,
> To take into the air my quiet breath;
> Now more than ever seems it rich to die,
> To cease upon the midnight with no pain,
> While thou art pouring forth thy soul abroad
> In such an ecstacy!
> Still wouldst thou sing, and I have ears in vain –
> To thy high requiem become a sod.
> (from *The Poems*, ed. Miriam Allott (Longman, London, 1970, p. 529))

'Darkling' (in darkness) recapitulates the previous stanza (starting 'I cannot see what flowers are at my feet') in which the darkness of the woods had seemed a luxurious and womblike experience. Now, the talk of death brings out the *ambivalence* of the earlier stanza. The phrases 'shadows numberless' and especially 'embalmed darkness' now seem more tomblike than womblike. The New Critic would dwell upon the complex implications of the poet's embrace of the idea of death. Death is an *escape* from the 'weariness, the fever, and the fret' of human existence which the nightingale's song had allowed the poet to forget. Death is 'easeful', and promises a gentle, painless dissolution. This is in tension with the poem's opening: 'My heart aches, and a drowsy numbness pains/My sense'. Life is more painful than the prospect of death. Many antinomies are in play around this tension between life and death: they are summed up in the poem's final question ('Do I wake or sleep?'). Secondly, death is realised both as a physical termination ('become a sod') and a religious experience. The release of the soul is concretely visualised in 'To take into the air my quiet breath'. The religious possibilities of the idea of being 'half in love' with death, the use of 'soft names' (like prayers), the accompanying spiritual ecstasy of the bird ('pouring forth thy soul') are sharpened and focused in 'thy high requiem', which takes us back to 'soft incense' and 'embalmed darkness' in stanza five. There is both an honest recognition of death's finality and an implication of spiritual ecstasy. The alternative views are left in suspension, and we are not free to resolve them into either blank despair or religious exaltation. Thirdly, the poet's sense that death is a rich experience depends upon his state of empathic union with the bird. He has achieved a perfectly self-effacing attentiveness to the beauty of the nightingale's song ('Darkling I listen'). Such a state is already a metaphorical death. The thought of death itself involves the thought of the end of sensual empathy ('I have ears in vain'). Hearing the bird gives rise to thoughts which threaten to destroy the possibility of hearing the bird. The knotty contradictoriness of this passage, along with its 'resonances' which reverberate throughout the poem, makes it a perfect illustration of Keats's own theory of negative capability. We are left, from a New Critical point of view, neither puzzled nor irritated by Keats's vagueness, but impressed by the richness, complexity and ambivalence of his vision.

This type of 'close reading' (usually called 'practical criticism') affirms a belief in the specificity and verbal density of poetry. One of the theoretical justifications for this view is summed up in the title of one of Brooks' essays – 'The Heresy of Paraphrase'. For the New Critics, poetic language cannot be translated into or reduced to prose statements. We cannot simply boil down Keats's poem to a few nuclear statements about life and death. To do so would remove all the poetic texture, which is not there simply to ornament the prose core of meaning but to convey the poet's realisation of a complex human response to life. In other words, to paraphrase a poem is to be guilty of a critical heresy. This theory provided critics with a new justification for detailed study of poetic language. The 'rhetorical' study of poetic figures, the classical form of 'close reading', analysed usage in order to tabulate the various possible devices of arrangement and expression. Poets studied rhetoric books in order to enhance their repertoire of effects. The New Critics followed the Romantics in regarding rhetoric as a merely external and prescriptive form of analysis. The former were concerned more with the special nature of poetic language and its *value* as a form of response to human experience. What reasons do contemporary critics have for rejecting New Criticism? As we have seen above, the humanism of the New Critics conceals a specific ideological form. Terry Eagleton has clarified the matter cogently:

> The literary text ... was grasped in what might be called 'functionalist' terms: just as American functionalist sociology developed a 'conflict-free' model of society, in which every element 'adapted' to every other, so the poem abolished all friction, irregularity and contradiction in the symmetrical cooperation of its various features. (*Literary Theory* p. 47)

A further common ground for the attack on New Criticism is its formalistic isolation of the literary text from its social, psychological and intertextual contexts. One of the attractions of formalism was that it gave criticism a distinct object of study. Critics could claim to have a specialist knowledge of texts which could not be provided by linguists, historians, sociologists or psychologists. The object of study was 'literary' language. As we shall see (in Chapter 2), Russian Formalists had already developed this position in a more rigorous and less subjective form. Most recent theories question the fundamental assumptions of formalism. 'Textuality' rather than the 'text' is the new object of study. That is, there is a wholesale rejection of the isolation of the text as an 'autotelic' object. Most modern theories address the question 'What are the structural conditions (linguistic, social, historical and psycho-sexual) which make possible particular forms of discourse?' Individual literary texts are no longer regarded as 'works', or as artfully constructed icons, or as distinct and separate objects. They are now conceived as discursive spaces through which all kinds of other texts and contexts criss-cross in an unstable web of significations. More of this later.

Section 3

Text: Henry James, *The Aspern Papers*
Theory: 'Rhetoric of Fiction' (Unreliable
Narrators)

The Chicago School of neo-Aristotelian criticism was an important
alternative to the New Criticism during the 1940s and 1950s. Its
exponents, who included R. S. Crane, W. R. Keast, Richard McKeon,
Elder Olson and Bernard Weinberg, believed that criticism had already
established a valid foundation in the fragmentary writings of Aristotle,
notably in the *Rhetoric* and *Poetics*. The Chicago School was scholarly,
systematic and theoretically sophisticated. It aimed to establish on a
firm philosophical foundation the principles which governed the whole
range of literary genres. Wayne C. Booth's study of the novelist's
techniques for imposing 'his fictional world upon the reader' is the
School's most influential text.

It was probably Plato who first pointed out that 'narration' can either
proceed by 'imitation' or 'simple narration' or by a mixture of the two.
When Homer describes in his own voice a hero's action this is 'simple
narration', but when he 'quotes' his hero's words this is 'imitation'. The
French structuralist Genette points out that this distinction is illusory
because in fact both types are part of a single narration; 'imitation' is
really just another form of narration. Nevertheless, if we think of
modern literature, it is evident that there is a clear difference between a
play and a novel in their mode of discourse. In a novel we can talk of
'narration' in the sense that a voice tells us a story, but in a play there is
no such narrative level (except when, within the play's structure, a
character narrates a story).

The confusion which might arise from these observations is avoided
if we make the necessary distinction between author and narrator.
There are novels (those of Henry Fielding and George Eliot, for
example) which appear to be narrated by their authors: the reader quite
naturally treats the 'voice' of the narrator as the author's, mainly

because the voice has all the authority of an author, and seems to possess a godlike knowledge of the characters. However, we can never really be certain that the attitudes of the narrator, even an omniscient narrator, are identical with those of the author. Wayne Booth argues, in *The Rhetoric of Fiction* (1961), that there is nevertheless a sense in which we recognise the values and attitudes of an author quite independently of our sense of the narrator's identity. He calls this sense of the author's voice the 'implied author' – an 'official scribe' or the author's 'second self'. This 'author' is not the actual author, but rather the author we construct by implication from the values expressed in the fiction.

This useful distinction leaves us free to talk about narration in its own right without losing ourselves in speculation about the author's attitudes. Booth uses the term 'rhetoric' to describe the study of fictional narration. Rhetoric, in the classical sense, is the study of verbal devices for the purpose of more effective speaking and writing. The 'rhetoric of fiction' studies the way in which writers construct their fictions in order to make them more effective in terms of narration. There is a whole range of narrators which an author may employ: at one extreme is the 'impersonal' narrator whose voice is not discernible as a separate identity and who characteristically speaks in the third person; at the other end of the spectrum is the 'unreliable' narrator who is usually a character in the story and who often uses the first person. At first sight, we might assume that the impersonal narrator is to be preferred as being able to give us a more faithful rendering of reality. However, we must remember, once more, that all narration is a construction behind which resides an 'implied author' who cannot be identified with the narrator. Impersonal narration does not guarantee greater objectivity or truth.

Henry James's *The Aspern Papers* (1888) is narrated by the central character of the story, a writer who inveigles his way into the Venetian home of an elderly lady and her niece in order to obtain by any means the 'Aspern papers' (correspondence in the possession of the elderly Miss Bordereau, who was admired by the fictional American poet, Jeffrey Aspern, whom James modelled on Byron). The narrator is unashamedly 'unreliable': he is morally quite without scruples and admits this to the reader ('there's no baseness I wouldn't commit for Jeffrey Aspern's sake'); and he has a limited and subjective view of the world he lives in. Henry James especially favoured this type of narrator who could not only provide a peculiar point of view but also convey that sense of 'bewilderment' which is more true to human experience than the omniscience of the conventional 'authorial' narrator. Our narrator, a 'publishing scoundrel', as Miss Bordereau calls him when she discovers him at night inspecting her secretaire in which he hopes the papers are kept, is a focus of uncertainty throughout the story. He frequently makes wrong deductions, confesses ignorance of the situation, or conveys a shifting perspective. His assumptions about the niece, Miss Tina, are proved quite mistaken. He regards her as essentially naïve and pitiful, and he has no scruples in seeking her help in defrauding her aunt. Having failed to establish any social contact with the ladies for many weeks, he is finally permitted to enter into conversation with Miss Tina at a time when her aunt is unwell. The narrator conveys his puzzlement:

> I scarce knew what to think of all this – of Miss Tina's sudden conversation to sociability and of the strange fact that the more the old woman appeared to decline to her end the less she should desire to be looked after. The story hung indifferently together, and I even asked myself if it mightn't be a trap laid for me, the result of a design to make me show my hand. I couldn't have told why my companions (as they could only by courtesy be called) should have this purpose – why they should try to trip up so lucrative a lodger. But at any hazard I kept on my guard, so that Miss Tina shouldn't have occasion again to ask me what I might really be 'up to'. Poor woman, before we parted for the night my mind was at rest as to what *she* might be [up to]. She was up to nothing at all.
> (This and the following passage from *The Aspern Papers and Other Stories*, ed. Adrian Poole (Oxford University Press, Oxford and New York, 1983, pp. 38–9))

The narrator turns out to be completely wrong. While he appears to be the plotter who is carefully and subtly achieving his aim, it turns out that the ladies are in fact the more effective plotters. They manage to persuade their lodger to pay exorbitantly for his lodgings, and it turns out that Miss Tina has a definite price in mind as payment for the papers. When the narrator realises that she wants him to marry her, he fails to conceal his revulsion, and he is defeated by Miss Tina's response: she destroys the papers and dismisses him.

The following passage suggests the wandering viewpoint of the narrator:

> I found myself mistakenly thinking of her too as one of Jeffrey Aspern's contemporaries; this came from her having so little in common with my own. It was possible, I indeed reasoned, that she hadn't even heard of him; it might very well be that Juliana [Bordereau] had forborne to lift for innocent eyes the veil that covered the temple of her glory [the papers]. In

this case she perhaps wouldn't know of the existence of the papers, and I welcomed that presumption – it made me feel more safe with her – till I remembered we had believed the letter of disavowal [sent earlier denying the existence of the papers] . . . to be in the handwriting of the niece.

James here evokes all the half-knowledge, false supposition, surface judgement and forgetfulness typical of most human consciousnesses. We are very far from the all-seeing clarity of the omniscient author who misses nothing and is never mistaken about the facts or about a character's thoughts. The unreliability of the narrator makes not only for comic irony (the 'publishing scoundrel' not only fails in his plot but is put in his place by the *naif*), but also produces a more 'truthful' rendering of human narrative consciousness.

Wayne Booth is surprisingly critical of James's use of the 'unreliable' narrator in this story. He points out that James, in his preface, indicates an intention to create a sense of the 'palpable imaginable *visitable* past'. Booth believes that the voice which tells us of this historical Venice is not compatible with the immoral and self-deceiving 'scoundrel' who narrates the story of his intended coup. Booth argues that this contradiction creates a kind of moral confusion which makes the story a failure. This presupposes that an artistic appreciation of the past is not psychologically compatible with lack of moral scruples of the kind illustrated in the story. It is by no means clear that this 'contradiction' is implausible. Booth's criticism of James certainly highlights the complexity produced by the use of unreliable narrators. In these cases the reader is forced to decide at what points the implied author's values can be separated from the narrator's. Is the concern for the Venetian past something we should attribute to James or to the narrator? Booth clearly attributes it to James and believes that James inartistically attributes it to the narrator.

An awareness of the types of narrative voice forearms us against naïvely blurring the distinction between authorial and non-authorial viewpoints. Beyond this, there remains the difficulty of locating precisely a 'reliable' focus of values and assumptions which will guide the reader's interpretation (see section 8 for further discussion). The limitations of Booth's work from a poststructuralist viewpoint lie precisely in this region.

Booth's book concludes with a brooding and inconclusive meditation upon the moral problems raised by the use of unreliable narrators. Booth is positively Johnsonian in his concern for the moral effects of particular techniques. An author, he argues, must be careful to communicate his own (ethically worthy) vision, and not allow unscrupulous, corrupt, deviant, or downright wicked characters too much scope to confuse the reader. Not all readers are capable of grasping the author's moral intentions. It is not hard to think of our own examples. There are many admirers of Milton's Satan, Graham Greene's whisky priest, Alf Garnett's racism and Loads-a-money's greed. Booth, in effect, argues that rhetorical techniques are successful only when they produce the intended moral identifications in readers.

Recent theories have cast doubt on several of Booth's working assumptions about reading and writing. Authors are no longer considered the sole arbiters of meaning: they transcribe and adapt the interminable discourses of culture and ideology in words which readers inevitably reinscribe with their own cultural and ideological systems of meaning. The model of the responsible author and the obediently responsive reader is now an antiquated one. However, the rhetoric of narration elaborated by Booth remains a useful source of concepts for a refashioned theory of literary discourse. On questions of point of view, types of narrator and especially the notion of the implied narrator, his work remains seminal.

Chapter 2

Russian Formalism

Section 4

Text: Laurence Sterne, *Tristram Shandy*
Theory: 'Baring the Device'

It is an old classical maxim that true art conceals its art (*ars celare artem*). According to this view, the best writing should try to efface the marks of the labour that went into it, and to give the appearance of spontaneous creativity. We admire what appears to have been done effortlessly rather than what seems laboured and achieved by constant revision and effort. The romantic poets added to this a new emphasis upon genuineness – 'the spontaneous overflow of powerful feeling' (Wordsworth's phrase is often quoted out of context in support of naïve Romantic ideas). To draw attention to one's art may seem to break the spell of the reader's identification with the poet: while we read we like to feel that we are hearing the poet's voice speaking to us intimately and with sincerity.

Another side of the same classical tradition stresses that art is artificial and that a great deal of acquired skill goes into it. There is an *art* of poetry. We can learn certain techniques and enlarge our repertoire of effects by studying the example of earlier great poets and dramatists. In classical poetics this technical attitude is combined with an almost religious admiration for the creative powers of great writers. The Romantics regarded the classical terms 'genius' and 'craft' as contradictory rather than complementary. Modern students of literature often follow the Romantics in preferring spontaneity to calculation. The passion of Ben Jonson's or Alexander Pope's poetry is lost on them, because it is too 'technical'.

Laurence Sterne's *Tristram Shandy* has a special place in the history of English literature: it is often cited as the first modernist novel, the first novel to consciously display its own technique. It is also an important precursor of the 'subjective' fiction of James Joyce and Virginia Woolf. At the end of his famous study of Sterne's novel (in

Russian Formalist Criticism (Lemon and Reis, 1965, pp. 25–57)) Victor Shklovsky declares: '*Tristram Shandy* is the most typical novel in world literature.' This odd remark only makes sense when placed in the context of the Russian Formalists' view of literature. They believed that critics should aim to establish a 'science' of literature – a complete knowledge of the formal effects (devices, techniques, etc.) which together make up what we call 'literature'. The *literary* aspects of poems, novels and plays are those which are concerned with transforming raw material (facts, emotions, stories, etc.) into literary works. People read literary texts for many reasons: for comfort, for inspiration, for entertainment. The Formalists read them in order to discover their 'literariness' – to highlight the devices and technical elements introduced by writers in order to make language literary. Shklovsky believed that literary devices 'defamiliarize' our perceptions of reality (see section 5).

Tristram Shandy is in many respects a special case, but from a Formalist point of view it is utterly typical. It is the most 'literary' of all novels in the sense that it is the most openly self-conscious in its 'baring' of novelistic devices. Indeed one could say that the novel's subject is its own devices. Sometimes this self-consciousness takes the form of parody: the conventions of the eighteenth-century novel are played upon unrelentingly. In giving us the 'Life and Opinions' of his hero Sterne mocks the artificial formula of the picaresque novel which tries to trace the picaro's life 'from birth to death'. He highlights this convention by exaggeration: we start with the precise moment of Tristram's conception – his father's interrupted ejaculation! Sterne parodies the novel's usual sequential pattern of chapters and preliminaries by transposing chapters, leaving one blank (to be filled in by the reader), and placing dedication and preface in the middle of the book. Thus the devices of the novel are 'laid bare'. This concept (laying bare the device) is used by Shklovsky to refer to Sterne's practice of presenting devices without any realistic 'motivation'; they are presented purely *as devices*. Shklovsky exaggerates this point at times, overlooking the central psychological motivations of Tristram's bizarre narration. Nevertheless, it remains true that Sterne's novel is an example of what modern theorists have called 'metafiction' – fiction about fiction.

Here is a typical passage:

> I will not finish that sentence till I have made an observation upon the strange state of affairs between the reader and myself, just as things stand at present – an observation never applicable before to any one biographic-

al writer since the creation of the world, but to myself – and I believe will never hold good to any other, until its final destruction – and therefore, for the very novelty of it alone, it must be worth your worships attending to.

I am this month one whole year older than I was this time twelve-month; and having got, as you perceive, almost into the middle of my fourth volume – and no farther than to my first day's life – 'tis demonstrative that I have three hundred and sixty-four days more life to write just now, than when I first set out; so that instead of advancing, as a common writer, in my work with what I have been doing at it – on the contrary, I am just thrown so many volumes back.

(From *The Life and Opinions of Tristram Shandy* (Oxford University Press, Oxford and New York, 1983, p. 228))

The appearance of chaos has the effect of drawing attention to the devices of fiction. It is possible in writing a novel to take a year to narrate the events and thoughts of a day. By slowing down the action Sterne not only exposes the devices of fiction but also defamiliarises time (see section 5 on defamiliarisation). The narrator draws attention to the strangeness of the writer's situation, but from a formalistic viewpoint the truth is the reverse. The state of affairs is quite typical of fiction: the time of narration bears no relation to real time. Fiction operates by distorting time in various ways – foreshortening, skipping, expanding, transposing, reversing, using flashback and flashforward, and so on. This distortion is an example of the very essence of the 'literariness' of fiction.

What are the limitations of this formalistic approach? First, it must be admitted that many of the devices which Shklovsky and the other Formalists isolated are not exclusively literary: they turn out to be used much more widely. Literary texts cannot be so easily differentiated from non-literary texts. This is an important matter, because some critics and linguists argue that the very existence of literary studies is put in question if the Formalists are proved wrong. This is going too far, I suggest, because we do not have to accept the Formalist's belief that literary study is exclusively about form and technique. It can be argued that the 'scientific' study of devices may well have a wider application, but that the study of *literary* devices as such remains justified, since literature provides the most concentrated examples of such techniques (as is clearly the case with Sterne).

Shklovsky's admiration for Sterne's thorough-going exposure of all the devices of eighteenth-century fiction anticipates contemporary critical interest in what Roman Jakobson called the 'metalingual' function of language. This refers to the 'codes' which underlie language and all sign systems. To explore the codes of eighteenth-century narratives would involve producing an inventory of its novelistic devices. By referring directly to this metalingual level Sterne is indicating his awareness of an existing set of conventions. This type of overt reference to the code being used is sometimes called 'self-reflexivity' or 'metafiction' (in the case of novels). Sterne anticipated a phenomenon which has become extremely common in twentieth-century literature. Novelists who show a preoccupation with the fictionality of their texts include David Lodge, B. S. Johnson, John Fowles, Vladimir Nabokov and Kurt Vonnegut. Modern consciousness itself is highly self-reflexive: we are often absorbed by the 'fictionality', the 'constructed' nature of our discourses, our institutions, and even our psychological identities. In this sense, to 'lay bare the device' is an act of modern authenticity.

Section 5

Texts: Craig Raine, 'A Martian Sends a Postcard Home', and William Golding, *The Inheritors*
Theory: 'Making Strange' (Defamiliarisation)

One view of language regards transparency as the ideal: words should represent things or ideas without drawing attention to their own materiality – their signifying substance. Bacon, the philosopher of science, believed that the mirror of the mind should reflect things without distortion and that words should transmit that perfect image of things. There is also a classical and literary version of Baconianism. It too believes that language can and should be tamed: metaphors and other literary devices should be subdued and rendered 'natural' and unobtrusive. Bad writers, according to this vision, are like bad gardeners: they allow language to grow luxuriant, to be overwhelmed with weeds of style which choke the healthy plants of truth and knowledge. The Augustan poets recognised that poetic language was not totally mirror-like, since poetry gives us an idealised and harmonious version of reality, but they still thought that poetry should transmit reality in its essential truth:

> But true expression, like th' unchanging sun,
> Clears and improves whate'er it shines upon,
> It gilds all objects, but it alters none.
> (Pope, *Essay on Criticism*, 315–17)

In this way the artificial and stylised poetic diction of the Augustans preserves the Baconian ideal of the mirror, or what the young Wittgenstein called the 'picture-view' of language.

The poetics of modernism was profoundly affected by Romantic and aestheticist traditions, and placed a new value upon linguistic technique. The Russian Formalists, especially Victor Shklovsky, developed a radical version of this view. Their arguments directed attention to the distinctive *linguistic* properties of literary language. Ordinary language, they argued, tends to diminish our awareness of reality: it simply confirms things as we know them. Ah yes, the leaves are falling from the trees; ah yes, the archer shoots an arrow at his target. All very familiar: the thoughts evoked by the words scarcely require dwelling upon or reflection. The reality they evoke is already in our possession; it needs no inspection. Such language, according to Shklovsky, encourages the automatisation of our perceptions: we take for granted a reality which is already fully *known* to us. Literary language and all other artistic forms work in the opposite direction: they draw attention to perceptions by making them *unfamiliar*.

It must be emphasised that Shklovsky was not interested in the *content* of perceptions, but only in the artistic defamiliarisation of them. To take an extreme example, a 'defamiliarised' artistic rendering of starving children in Africa would draw attention to the *perception* (close-up, montage, detail) but not to the moral or political issues. In this respect he differed fundamentally from Bertolt Brecht who used the 'alienation effect' to alter the perceptions of the theatre audience. Many of the examples given by Shklovsky involve an unusual point of view or narrator. If the writer uses a horse as narrator (Tolstoy does this in *Kholstomer*) there is a guaranteed effect of strangeness, because nothing can be left automatically represented; everything must be dwelt upon and described as if for the first time. Craig Raine's 'A Martian Sends a Postcard Home' has an equally unusual narrator:

Caxtons are mechanical birds with many wings
and some are treasured for their markings –

they cause the eyes to melt
or the body to shriek without pain.

I have never seen one fly, but
sometimes they perch on the hand.

Mist is when the sky is tired of flight
and rests its soft machine on ground:

then the world is dim and bookish
like engraving under tissue paper.

Rain is when the earth is television.
It has the property of making colours darker.

Model T is a room with the lock inside –
a key is turned to free the world

for movement, so quick there is a film
to watch for anything missed.

But time is tied to the wrist
or kept in a box, ticking with impatience.

In homes, a haunted apparatus sleeps,
that snores when you pick it up.

If the ghost cries, they carry it
to their lips and soothe it to sleep

with sounds. And yet, they wake it up
deliberately, by tickling with a finger.

Only the young are allowed to suffer
openly. Adults go to a punishment room

with water but nothing to eat.
They lock the door and suffer the noises

alone. No one is exempt
and everyone's pain has a different smell.

At night, when all the colours die,
they hide in pairs

and read about themselves –
in colour, with their eyelids shut.

(From *A Martian Sends a Postcard Home* (Oxford University Press,
Oxford, 1979))

One of the problems about Shklovsky's discussions of Tolstoy and Swift
is the fact that he blatantly ignores their moral purposes. Raine's poem
requires no such one-sidedness. Unlike Tolstoy's horse or Swift's giant
in Lilliput, the Martian is a narrator without social conscience. He
observes an entirely personal and private world: the reading of books,
the weather, driving fast cars, wearing wrist watches, using the
telephone and the WC, and dreaming. It is also clear that Raine is not
primarily interested in changing our perceptions about these personal
experiences and commonplaces. He is interested in their *defamiliarisation*. The narrator perceives the reading of books in two completely
discontinuous frames of reference, one metonymic and the other
metaphoric (see section 9 on these figures): 'Caxton' is *associated* with
books through the invention of the printing press, while birds *resemble*
books in their moving pages and beautiful markings. By perceiving
books as perching on hands Raine adds nothing to our sense of reality,
but rather dwells artistically and formalisticly upon the perception for
its own sake. The 'making strange' of the telephone (seeing it as a baby)
involves an incongruous animation of the inanimate: 'haunted',
'sleeps', 'snores', 'ghost cries', 'soothe it to sleep', 'wake it up/
deliberately, by tickling with a finger' operate a device aimed not at
teaching us something we didn't know about phones but at giving us a
different, unfamiliar perception of using telephones. It stops us for a

moment passing over our already established mental image of a commonplace experience, but the concern is purely with the poetic effect. Raine is concerned with what the Russian Formalists called 'literariness' (see section 4) – the devices which distinguish literary from non-literary language (or appear to). The clue to Raine's formalism lies in his evident lack of concern to establish any psychological or cognitive coherence in the Martian discourse. The Martian appears to know of certain things, names and concepts (Caxton, engravings, TV, film, Model T, punishment), but to be ignorant of others (books, cars, telephones, WCs). He doesn't know that people are talking down their telephones, but does know that they have dreams. He doesn't understand reading books but he has a concept of people reading 'about themselves – in colour'. It is possible to see the poet's point of view lurking behind the Martian's. The latter's category mistakes might suggest that human life has become a technological prison, the only escape from which is found in dreams. Nevertheless, Raine seems more interested in the *formal* effects of the 'misunderstandings'.

William Golding uses the device of defamiliarisation with a psychological and cognitive purpose in *The Inheritors*, his novel about Neanderthal man. In the second part of the novel, after the perceptual world of Lok and his group have been thoroughly established, we are given sudden views and descriptions of Cro-Magnon man (the 'new people') seen through the eyes of Lok and others. Here is Lok's description of an arrow being shot at him:

> The man had white bone things above his eyes and under the mouth so that his face was longer than a face should be. The man turned sideways in the bushes and looked at Lok along his shoulder. A stick rose upright and there was a lump of bone in the middle. Lok peered at the stick and the lump of bone and the small eyes in the bone things over the face. Suddenly Lok understood that the man was holding the stick out to him but neither he nor Lok could reach across the river. He would have laughed if it were not for the echo of the screaming in his head. The stick began to grow shorter at both ends. Then it shot out to full length again.
> The dead tree by Lok's ear acquired a voice.
> 'Clop!'
> His ears twitched and he turned to the tree. By his face there had grown a twig. . . .
> (From *The Inheritors* (Faber and Faber, London, 1955, 1961, p. 106))

It is not until near the end of the novel that we have a description of Lok from the point of view of the new people: 'It was a strange creature, smallish and bowed.' Earlier we had seen ourselves (the new people) through Lok's eyes: 'The new people did not move like anything he had ever seen before. They were balanced on the top of their legs. . . . They did not look at the earth but straight ahead.' Lok's perception of the bowman is similarly established in 'his face was longer than a face should be'. The defamiliarised firing of the arrow, unlike Raine's defamiliarised reading of a book, is concerned with establishing a world-view – Neanderthal man's. The pointing of the bow towards Lok can be understood only as an offering gesture, which puzzles Lok because the intervening river makes such a gesture impractical. The visual illusion of the bow's (fore-)shortening cannot be read accurately by Lok, since he has no experience of offensive weapons. Even the arrival of the arrow is translated into a speaking tree and a sudden growth of a twig – events which are part of a mythopoeic and magical view of the universe.

Shklovsky would have found Golding's technique exemplary, but would not have been interested in its ideological or moral purpose. The slowing down of the perception and the 'roughening' of the textual surface are sufficient reason for the effect of defamiliarisation. Golding is thereby doing what a creative writer should do – producing literary discourse by deploying various devices. From a non-formalist point of view a Shklovskian approach to defamiliarisation provides a more complete interpretation of Raine's writing than Golding's. Raine's concern with formal effects is probably an indication of his desire to avoid larger social and historical questions. Golding is trying to present a Neanderthal discourse, and thereby a Neanderthal world-view and experience. In both cases the Formalist approach is useful in drawing attention to *technique*. It is possible, by following the example of Brecht, to see how one might find moral or political uses for Formalist ideas. Instead of merely asking what artistic effects are gained by the use of devices such as defamiliarisation, we can ask what ideological effects are produced by such devices. In other words, Formalism can be liberated from its merely technical constraints.

Chapter 3

Structuralism

Section 6

Text: Christopher Smart, *Jubilate Agno*
Theory: Naturalisation

No piece of language can be said to have a 'meaning' until it has been understood by a reader or a listener. When we are confronted with words we are compelled to interpret them. It may often seem as though the words need no interpretation at all: their meaning may seem to be written on their faces, so to speak. To take the celebrated example of British Rail's notice on its WCs – 'Gentlemen lift the seat' – it is perfectly obvious that the message could be interpreted in several ways:

1. Gentlemen [as opposed to those of a lesser status, can be relied on to] lift the seat [when urinating].
2. Gentlemen [, please] lift [only] the seat!
3. Gentlemen [,] lift the seat [of your trousers].
4. Upper-class gents are invited to steal the seat.

Invent your own interpretation! The 'correct' one is not difficult to discover, simply because when we interpret public notices we obey certain rules or conventions. It is possible, of course, to produce a notice which is ambiguous, as sometimes happens in the case of English translations of foreign notices, but this defeats the whole purpose of such uses of language.

When we come to the interpretation of literary texts, according to many structuralist critics, we are faced with a similar situation. A text or piece of text could be made to mean many different things by different readers. Literary texts are more likely to give rise to variable interpretation than non-literary texts. They are often designed to allow the reader to 'produce' a rich vein of interpretation. However, this does not mean that interpretation is therefore completely subjective and impressionistic, because, as in the case of our British Rail notice, interpretations are produced within a set of rules or conventions. Jonathan Culler argues (in *Structuralist Poetics*, 1975) that a structuralist theory of criticism should aim to explain how readers actually manage to produce meanings from texts. He believes that the 'structure' resides not in the texts themselves but *the set of rules we follow* (unconsciously perhaps) when we read (see also section 16).

The Dadaists (an anarchic group of artists and writers working between 1916 and 1920) were committed to rejecting all conventions of meaning. The classic Dadaist poem is produced totally at random (words taken from a hat) in order to forestall any possible conventionality of form, rhythm or meaning. However, what is interesting about even this extreme case is that, if we are presented with a Dadaist poem, the natural thing to do is to interpret it. It is built into a reader's acquired responses to try to make sense of everything and to find sense even in non-sense. Of course, throughout literary history major writers have produced works which have been regarded as nonsense by readers unfamiliar with the developed reading practices demanded by innovative texts. However, the assumption remains that all literary works should be readable in principle, and that, if a work resists the reader's efforts to make sense of it, the writer is at fault. A more sophisticated response to this problem is to say that the readers have to be patient with innovative writings and try to discover the mode of reading which the texts demand. To return to our Dadaist poem, many readers, especially those who have acquired, to use Culler's term, 'literary competence' (see section 16), will try to find a meaning even in a totally random text.

There are several ways in which we 'naturalise' literary texts and make them part of a recognisable universe of meaning. First, there is an appeal to verisimilitude; we interpret a text as merely stating what is 'really' the case – the way things are. This is related to the idea that a text speaks of accepted knowledge – attitudes and ideas which are part of common knowledge (for example, the notion that academics are absent-minded). Next, there are the conventions which a particular work observes and by which the reader interprets. We have no difficulty in understanding references to strange creatures with two heads invading the world if we are reading science fiction. More generally, we allow ourselves to absorb the atmosphere and point of view of a fiction we are reading; we try to interpret everything according to the special viewpoint which the text provides. Sometimes, more interestingly, a writer will take a certain set of conventions (pastoral, lyric, heroic, realistic and so on) and subvert, question or parody them. The reader has to grasp this double level in order to read the poem as 'natural'. These, then, are a few of the forms of 'naturalisation' which a reader may employ. The essential point is that readers always look for some sort of coherence however bizarre or fragmented it may be. If we are told that a piece of text is 'poetry', we naturalise it according to a different set of expectations from those we would apply to prose. Readers who have acquired 'literary competence' will attend to poetry in a much more specific and detailed manner than they would in the case of a paragraph from a newspaper. Such elements as line-endings, assonance, repetition, word-order, internal line balance, and so on will take on potential significance. We do not assume that a poem will yield its meaning directly as if it were a piece of natural language. When we read it, we recuperate it and restore it to a natural state of meaning by reading it as poetry. As Culler shows, the poeticalness lies not in the poem as much as in the conventions which operate when we read on the assumption that a text is a piece of poetry.

Christopher Smart, the eighteenth-century poet, was an established classical scholar and fellow of Pembroke College, Cambridge, but between 1757 and 1763 he was placed in confinement on several occasions because he was suffering from a compulsive mental illness which took the form of religious mania; he insisted on praying in public and trying to involve others in his prayers. During his confinement he composed a long religious 'poem' called *Jubilate Agno* ('Rejoice in the Lamb'). Here is an extract from the poem:

> Let Barsabas rejoice with Cammarus – Newton is ignorant for if a man consult not the WORD how should he understand the WORK?
> For there is infinite provision to keep up the life in all the parts of Creation.
>
> Let Lydia rejoice with Attilus – Blessed be the name of him which eat the fish and honey comb.
> For the AIR is contaminated by curses and evil language.
>
> Let Jason rejoice with Alopecias, who is subtlety without offence.
> For poisonous creatures catch some of it and retain it or ere it goes to the adversary.
>
> Let Dionysius rejoice with Alabes who is peculiar to the Nile.
> For IRELAND was without these creatures, till of late, because of the simplicity of the people.
>
> Let Damaris rejoice with Anthias – the fountain of the Nile is known to the Eastern people who drink it.
> For the AIR is purified by prayer which is made aloud and with all our might.

Let Apollos rejoice with Astacus, but St Paul is the Agent for England.
For loud prayer is good for weak lungs and for a vitiated throat.

Let Justus rejoice in a Salmon-Trout – the Lord look on the soul of
Richard Atwood.
For SOUND is propagated in the spirit and in all directions.

Let Crispus rejoice with Leviathan – God be gracious to the soul of
HOBBES, who was no atheist, but a servant of Christ, and died in the
Lord – I wronged him God forgive me.
For the VOICE of a figure is complete in all its parts.

Let Aquila rejoice with Beemoth who is Enoch, no fish but a stupendous
creeping Thing.
For a man speaks HIMSELF from the crown of his head to the sole of his
feet. [. . .]

Let Gaius rejoice with the Water-Tortoise – Paul and Tychicus were in
England with Agricola my father.
For all whispers and unmusical sounds in general are of the Adversary.
(From *The Poetical Works of Christopher Smart*, vol. I, ed. Karina
Williamson (Clarendon Press, Oxford, 1980))

Some readers might regard this as pure nonsense or, at best, as
deranged. It appears to be a muddle of biblical, contemporary, and
private allusion, jumbled into a curiously mechanical patterned form.
However, a reader who has mastered the skill involved in reading
poetry will be able to get further. The first thing we look for in poetry is
pattern. In reading prose we move generally from one thing to another
in a *sequence*, but in poetry we look for *equivalences* – elements in the
poetry which link similar features. The most obvious feature (in some
cases) is rhyme: rhyming words are equivalent in sound. The Smart
poem has no rhyme, and, of course, a good deal of modern poetry lacks
this particular feature too. However, the absence of rhyme links the
poem not with free verse in the modern sense but with the verse forms
of the Old Testament. Smart has written his poem in the form of
canticles (church hymns based on biblical texts). The element of
pattern is present in the 'antiphonal' praise and response pattern – 'Let'
and 'For'. We therefore read each 'Let' and each 'For' as *equivalent* to
the next.

This type of recognition is, of course, very simple, and hardly
adequate as a way of describing poetic reading. Culler suggests that
there are further assumptions which we often bring to our reading. The
three central assumptions are those of unity, significance and impersonality. That is, we assume that the text will be unified by various
possible elements, that it will be focused by a poetic significance which

will go beyond mere utilitarian meaning, and that the speaker of the poem is not reducible to the private voice of the poet. Finally, does the process of 'naturalisation' discussed above apply to poetry? In one sense, poetry seems to defy naturalisation, because it so often departs from familiar prose usage, but in another, its deviance actually demands naturalisation. When we read poetry we apply strategies for recuperating difficult or unfamiliar pieces of writing. A central strategy is to make *figurative transformations*. That is, when we come up against a statement which defies common sense we naturalise it by reading it metaphorically or according to some other figure of speech.

How do the various assumptions and strategies involved in reading a text 'as poetry' operate in the case of Smart's poem? First the principle of equivalence guides us to see that the links between the 'Let' statements and those between the 'For' statements are more important than those between the 'Let' and 'For' statements. This means that the normal syntactical expectations are frustrated: the conjunction 'for' would normally introduce a statement which supports with arguments a preceding statement. We seek in vain for meaningful connections between 'Let' and 'For' statements, but the links between the equivalent statements are very strong. The 'For' sentences develop an independent line of thought: Life > Air > Purification > Prayer > Lungs > Sound, etc. By pursuing these links we arrive at two simple propositions: (1) the air, which is contaminated by evil language, may be purified by fervent prayer; (2) a strong and musical sound is holy, while whispers and discordant noises are from Satan. In contrast the 'Let' statements are apparently static and without development. Each of them exhorts a person (all the names in this extract are drawn from Acts) to rejoice in a particular fish (the Latin names are mostly drawn from the Roman naturalist Pliny). Thus the opening clauses of the 'Let' statements emphasise equivalence and are all based on the same structure (Let 'X' rejoice in 'Y'), while the remaining clause(s) are non-formulaic and varied in syntax and register.

The reader's attempts to apply figurative transformations to the poem's images produce a striking effect: all metaphors turn into literal statements. We might say that a curse contaminates the air, intending a purely metaphorical significance, but in Smart's 'For the AIR is contaminated by curses and evil language' air is literally contaminated. The statement involves metonymy (see also section 8) not metaphor: the soul expresses itself in words which infect or purify the air as they are emitted. Any physical weaknesses in the organs of speech are made better by the passage through them of 'prayer'. The ruling figure is metonymy, because meaning is governed by the *context* (spirit, prayer, words, throat, air). One element in the context stands for another: words (or sound) stand for the spirit; weak lungs stand for a defective person. The line 'For there is infinite provision to keep up the life in all the parts of Creation' stresses the interconnectedness of all things: each thing can stand for all the rest.

My discussion of 'literary competence' has, I hope, shown that reading is only apparently spontaneous, and that it brings into play strategies and concepts which help to recuperate difficult texts and to naturalise them. This approach is in sharp contrast to the Russian Formalists' concept of defamiliarisation (see section 2). They argued that literary language makes the familiar 'strange' by slowing down or otherwise disrupting automatised perceptions. The concept of naturalisation makes it possible for us to see that defamiliarised perceptions may be accommodated to different reading strategies.

This concept is useful in theorising a certain kind of ideological process. Marxist and poststructuralist critics tend to use the term 'recuperate' (rather than naturalise) to describe the way in which deviant or non-conforming elements in a literary text are smoothly taken into a dominant discourse, contained, and thereby prevented from becoming truly subversive. For example, Lear's speeches on behalf of 'poor naked wretches' (see section 24), who roam the countryside unsheltered and unfed, can be read as a radical attack upon Elizabethan social policy, or they can be 'recuperated' by a humanist discourse which reads the speeches as 'universal' Christian statements about the need for charity. This structuralist concept helps us to understand how particular ways of reading can support particular forms of ideology.

Section 7

Text: Arthur Miller, *Death of a Salesman*
Theory: Binary Oppositions

'Binary Oppositions' (BOs) are fundamental to structuralist thought. They also appear to be fundamental not only to human thought in general but even in some cases to the natural order itself. Consider the following BOs:

Masculine/Feminine
Night/Day
Black/White
Open/Closed
Straight/Crooked
High/Low

The list does not contain uniformly equivalent BOs. We confidently assign the first two to the natural order, while the others are less 'natural' and more 'cultural'. However, feminists have challenged the apparently 'natural' masculine/feminine BO, arguing that it is a cultural opposition. Certainly one must agree that a very large part of the content of this BO is cultural: the attributes we assign to each term (masculine = strong, feminine = submissive, and so on) are not universal but culturally variable. The biological distinction male/female is only a small part of the cultural BO. It is equally obvious that 'night' and 'day' take on a wide range of cultural meanings (evil/good, and so on) and thereby become 'signs'.

Forms of binarism are present in human thought from the earliest times. Dualisms in philosophy and religion (subject and object, God and man, mind and external world, organic and mechanical, temporal and eternal, and so on) are the very foundations of entire world-views. The concept of 'privatives' is also important in this context. We can describe the world in terms of the *absence* of certain qualities. Darkness is an absence of light; the iron is cold when it lacks heat; an object is still when it lacks movement. The concept of privatives can invade certain substantive BOs. For example, as feminists have pointed out, 'woman' is often defined as lacking certain male features (notably the penis). Deconstructive critics (see sections 12 and 14) are particularly interested in the pervasive presence of binary logic in Western discourse (especially the dualisms referred to above).

Structuralists have argued that binary oppositions are fundamental to human language, cognition and communication. We use BOs to mark *differences* in an otherwise apparently random sequence of features, and thus to give shape to our experience and to the universe. Why 'binary' and not 'ternary'? Take, for example, the case of traffic lights. The system usually requires three terms: RED/AMBER/GREEN. Is this essentially ternary? Well, the problem is that AMBER is subordinate in its function to the other two colours. AMBER means 'prepare for red or green'. The fundamental opposition is binary: stop/go.

The structuralist linguist Roman Jakobson showed that we identify a phoneme (the smallest meaningful unit of sound) by using (unconsciously) a number of BOs which make it possible to differentiate between otherwise similar sounds (see *Fundamentals of Language*, 1971, Part 1, pp. 13–17, 38–44). We distinguish 'puck' from 'buck' because the BO 'voice/unvoiced' makes it possible to distinguish between two 'plosives' (/p/ is 'unvoiced', /b/ is 'voiced'). What would otherwise be heard as the 'same' sound is heard as 'different'. Subsequently, this insight was applied by structuralists to literary structures in which units of meaning above the level of 'phoneme' were sought. It is important to note that in literary structuralism the principle of phonemic difference is used as a general *model* of structure and not as an analytic method. For example, Lévi-Strauss pointed out the 'phonemic' patterns (systems of mythemes) underlying particular myths. The mythemes are distinctive events in the mythic story which can be arranged in binary pairs to form a system of cultural meanings (see *Structural Anthropology*, 1963, chapter 11). Critics of Lévi-Strauss have rejected his method on the grounds that he tries to elevate a reading method to an objective science.

Jonathan Culler, in his *Structuralist Poetics* (1975), questions the possibility of discovering binary structures in texts, and concentrates on the reader's use of BOs as a means of attributing significance to literary texts. The discovery of BOs is one of the central strategies of reading and interpretation. Appearance and reality, Heaven and Earth, court and town, country and city, body and soul, reason and feeling, high and low, are a few of the many BOs which readers have employed as interpretive strategies. However, Culler warns us that the primary danger of BOs is that they permit one to classify anything: we can always find some difference between any two items. This is especially dangerous when we are tempted to align two BOs and to regard them as 'homologous' (possessing the same structure) merely because they are both present in a text. However, certain BOs are capable of generating a whole series of associated oppositions within a text. This applies, for example, to the organic and mechanical (D. H. Lawrence), biological nature and Divine Nature (Shakespeare) and fancy and judgement (Alexander Pope).

Arthur Miller's *Death of a Salesman* (1949) concerns the Loman family. Willy is a failed salesman whose sons, Biff and Happy, are also failures largely through their father's bad influence. The play concludes with Willy's suicide. The great American Dream is embodied in Willy's dead brother Ben who went into the jungle at 18 and came out very rich at 21 and appears to Willy from time to time in the play. The Lomans' lack of business success is paralleled by moral failures. Biff's prospects are ruined early by petty thieving, which Willy makes light of, reassuring Biff that what matters is having the right image and being 'well thought of'. Neither Biff (at 34) nor Happy are married, and Willy had a sexual affair when Biff was 17. Happy's sexual promiscuity is linked to his envy of others' success:

> *Happy.* But take those two we had tonight. Now weren't they gorgeous creatures?
> *Biff.* Yeah, yeah, most gorgeous I've had in years.
> *Happy.* I get that any time I want, Biff. Whenever I feel disgusted. The only trouble is, it gets like bowling or something. I just keep knockin' them over and it doesn't mean a thing. You still run around a lot?
> *Biff.* Naa. I'd like to find a girl – steady, somebody with substance.
> *Happy.* That's what I long for.
> *Biff.* Go on! You'd never come home.
> *Happy.* I would! Somebody with character, with resistance! Like Mom, y'know? You're gonna call me a bastard when I tell you this. That girl Charlotte I was with tonight is engaged to be married in five weeks . . . the guy's in line for the vice-presidency of the store. I don't know what gets into me, maybe I just have an overdeveloped sense of competition or something, but I went and ruined her.

(This and the following extracts from *Death of a Salesman* (The Viking Press, New York, 1949, pp. 24–5, 91–2, 95–6))

Happy's inability to compete in the hard business world makes him want to succeed ruthlessly and heartlessly in the world of sex. The emptiness of this endless 'scoring' does not lead him to question the ethics of the market-place. A different link between sex and business is made when we learn that Biff discovered Willy's infidelity at the time he flunked his exams. The shock prevented him from trying to resist them and ultimately caused his failure to establish a career.

Willy's neighbour Charley is a successful businessman who keeps Willy going financially. Willy's pride prevents him from accepting a job offer from Charley. Charley's son Bernard was a swot when Biff was at school but has become a successful lawyer. Willy had called him 'anemic' as a boy compared with the athletic Biff. It turns out that Bernard had been feeding Biff with examination answers (rather as his father Charley had fed Willy cash which Willy pretended he was earning himself). In Act 2 Willy meets the adult Bernard at Charley's office where Willy has gone to get more money from Charley:

> Bernard. What's Biff doing?
> Willy.   Well, he's been doing very big things in the West. But he
>   decided to establish himself here. Very big. We're having
>   dinner. Did I hear your wife had a boy?
> Bernard. That's right. Our second.
> Willy.   Two boys! What do you know!
> Bernard. What kind of deal has Biff got?
> Willy.   Well, Bill Oliver – very big sporting-goods man – he wants Biff
>   very badly. Called him from the West. Long distance, carte
>   blanche, special deliveries. Your friends have their own private
>   tennis court?
> Bernard. You still with the old firm, Willy?
> Willy.   [after a pause] I'm – I'm overjoyed to see how you made the
>   grade, Bernard, overjoyed. It's an encouraging thing to see a
>   young man really – really – Looks very good for Biff – very – [he
>   breaks off, then] Bernard – [he is so full of emotion, he breaks off
>   again.]
> Bernard. What is it, Willy?
> Willy.   [small and alone] What – what's the secret?

Willy's empty big talk breaks down before Bernard's modest silence. Bernard, like Willy, has two boys, but Willy's feckless sons have no children. Later, Charley embarrasses his son by mentioning that Bernard is flying to Washington to argue a case in front of the Supreme Court. After Bernard leaves the room, Willy expresses his 'shocked, pained and happy' reaction:

> Willy.   [as Charley takes out his wallet] The Supreme Court! And he
>   didn't even mention it!
> Charley. [counting out money on the desk] He don't have to – he's gonna
>   do it.

Willy.   And you never told him what to do, did you? You never took
any interest in him.

Charley.   My salvation is that I never took any interest in anything.

The Big Talk of the Lomans increases with their failure. Conversely
Charley's parental silence and Bernard's modesty coincide with Big
Success. 'Taking interest' is negative, while 'taking no interest' is
positive. The patterns of contrast and similarity between the characters
turn upon certain qualitatively significant binary oppositions, which
have been active all the time in my analysis thus far. The BOs are
apparent in key correlations between (1) morality and success, (2) talk
(or dream) and success. Moral failures correlate with career failures; the
amount of talk or dream is in inverse proportion to career success. Each
term has a positive and a negative value (morality or immorality,
success or failure, dream and talk or their opposites). We can express
the BOs as they relate to particular characters as follows:

(A)	Willy sexual immorality		Biff career failure
	Happy sexual immorality		Happy career failure
	Biff immorality (theft)		Biff career failure
(B)	Willy talk		Willy career failure
	Bernard no talk		Bernard career success
	Willy dreaming		Lomans career failure
	Charley no dreaming		Bernard career success

These patterns can be reduced further to a few abstract binary
oppositions:

+immorality		−immorality	
+dream	−success	−dream	+success
+talk		−talk	

I do not pretend to have found all the possible BOs which might
produce significances from the play's textual signifiers. The demonstration merely shows that our attempts to discover meaning are often
based upon binary patterns. We have followed Culler's view in

regarding the BOs as reading strategies rather than textual features. This orientation of structuralism not only anticipates the moves of deconstruction but also has a great deal in common with reader–response types of criticism (see especially section 16).

Section 8

Text: John Updike, 'Should Wizard Hit Mommy?'
Theory: Narrative Theory (especially structuralist)

Here is the opening of John Updike's story 'Should Wizard Hit Mommy?':

> In the evenings and for Saturday naps like today's, Jack told his daughter Jo a story out of his head. This custom, begun when she was two, was itself now nearly two years old, and his head felt empty. Each new story was a slight variation of a basic tale: a small creature, usually named Roger (Roger Fish, Roger Squirrel, Roger Chipmunk), had some problem and went with it to the wise old owl. The owl told him to go to the wizard, and the wizard performed a magic spell that solved the problem, demanding in payment a number of pennies greater than the number Roger Creature had but in the same breath directing the animal to a place where the extra pennies could be found. Then Roger was so happy he played many games with other creatures, and went home to his mother just in time to hear the train whistle that brought his daddy home from Boston. Jack described their supper, and the story was over.
>
> (From *Pigeon Feathers and Other Stories* (Alfred A. Knopf, New York, 1963, pp. 74–5))

The rest of the short story tells how on this occasion Jo steps out of her passive role as listener and begins to assert her own will over the story: she decides that the creature this time is going to be 'Roger Skunk'; she prompts Jack at the various stages in the tale (seeing the owl, being sent to the wizard); and finally she rejects Jack's version of the tale's ending. If we are reading the story for its psychological insights or its 'truth value', we might say that it illustrates the transition from innocence to experience; Jo is entering 'a reality phase' (as Jack – or the narrator – notes). She wants the story she is told to suit her own needs and desires, and therefore she rejects her father's version (which reflects *his* needs and desires). This account of the story is fine as far as it goes, but if we examine it from the point of view of narrative theory (and especially structuralist types of theory) we will be able to give a fuller account in certain respects.

62   *Practising Theory and Reading Literature*

The structuralist assumption is that all stories can be reduced to certain essential narrative structures. This notion is based on the related idea that all particular linguistic utterances (spoken or written) are based upon a 'language system' or grammar which is capable of producing a virtually infinite corpus of utterances. The system itself does not have a separate existence, but is deducible from actual utterances. Ferdinand de Saussure, whose linguistic theories influenced structuralism, called the system 'langue' and utterance 'parole'. There are many aspects to a structuralist theory of narrative (and many versions). They include three main dimensions:

1. Thematic structure.
2. Linear structure (the sequence of actions).
3. The structure of narration (how the story is communicated).

If we consider the second for a moment, we can say that most structuralist theories try to reduce to a manageable size the number of narrative 'functions' which can be used in stories to form a sequence of actions. Vladimir Propp, in his *Morphology of the Folktale* (1928), found thirty-one 'functions' in the corpus of Russian tales he studied. He showed that all the tales used some of the functions, and always in the same order. The last two are 'The Villain is punished' and 'The Hero is married and ascends the throne'. Structuralists later tried to produce a typology of functions for more general use. The simplest formulation is that of Claude Bremond who describes the logical sequence of narrative functions as follows:

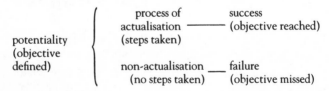

Using Bremond's scheme (as modified by S. Rimmon-Kenan, *Narrative Fiction*, 1983, p. 22) we can see that Jack's stories always have the same structure:

objective	– steps taken	– success
(to solve 'problem')	(consult wizard)	(problem solved)

The alternatives ('no steps taken' and 'failure') are not used. This analysis makes it clear that Jack's story formula with its exclusion of conflict is suited to very young children. This is also apparent if we use

A. J. Greimas's well-known scheme which focuses on characters in narrative in terms of six *actants* as follows:

<table>
<tr><td>sender</td><td>–</td><td>object</td><td>–</td><td>receiver</td></tr>
<tr><td>helper</td><td>–</td><td>subject</td><td>–</td><td>opponent</td></tr>
</table>

Greimas developed what he called a 'structural semantics' which involved treating narratives as if there were sentences (see *Structural Semantics*, 1983). *Actants* work like nouns and are general categories which underlie all narratives. A character or an object may take on the role of one or more *actants*, and more than one character or object can function as one *actant*. In Jack's story formula Roger Creature is the Subject (hero), his Object is a solution to the 'problem', the Receiver is also Roger, the Helper is the Wizard (the owl is a subsidiary helper) and there is no Opponent (or villain).

The schemes of Bremond and Greimas require great elaboration to make them work sensitively, but their ambitious aim is clear – they try to show the underlying structure of all narratives. The danger of such approaches is that the results may seem obvious or banal. However, the analysis of Jack's story becomes more interesting when we consider the development of Updike's tale. Jack, having provided a basic story structure (what we might call an 'empty' structure to be filled with various contents), finds himself forced by Jo to fill it in a certain way. First, Jo repeatedly prompts Jack, starting by suggesting the name of the hero – 'Roger Skunk'. Roger's problem is, of course, his smell which leaves him without playmates. Jo reminds Jack of the visits to the Owl and then to the Wizard. The cure is effected, payment is made and Roger, now smelling beautifully of roses, is able to have a wonderful time playing with friends. Jo is obviously satisfied and thinks the story is over, but Jack, not wanting her to take things for granted, inserts a new type of ending: back at home Mommy is very upset about Roger's transformation, drags Roger back to the Wizard, hits the Wizard on the head with her umbrella, and makes him restore Roger's skunk smell. The story then continues as usual with father's return from work and a lovely dinner. Jo is outraged and reminds her father that the other animals will now shun Roger; but Jack stubbornly defends Mommy against Jo's complaints ('That was a stupid mommy'), threatening her with a spanking if she doesn't settle down and go to sleep.

We can now see that the story of Roger Skunk can be analysed, using Bremond and Greimas, in two different ways. From Jo's viewpoint the movement from Objective through Actualisation to Success is re-versed: the story ends with Roger facing the same problem and running the risk of having no playmates. In her version Mommy is the Opponent (villain). Jo's story is a sort of Tragedy. From Jack's viewpoint the plot ends happily: the Objective is harmony between Mommy (and Daddy) and Roger, and it is actualised by Mommy's action in returning to the Wizard; Mommy is the Helper, the Wizard the Opponent. From this we can see that the same story can be analysed in two quite different ways using the same structural scheme.

It seems to me that this narrative analysis is helpful in drawing attention to aspects of the story which go beyond narrative theory. We begin to see that Jack and Jo have some kind of emotional and psychological investment in their particular interpretations of the story. It might seem that Jack's interpretation must be right, since he is the storyteller. However, not only does Jo exercise a good deal of influence on the story but she seems perfectly aware of the *convention-ality* of the story. She draws attention to her father's slip when he calls Roger 'Roger Fish' (she understands that each story is a retelling of the same story), and she responds to sad bits in the story with a conventional sadness: 'Jo made the crying face again, but this time without a trace of sincerity.' Because she is able to treat the story as a narrative structure and not as an absolute reality she is able to question the storyteller ('the source of truth') and to contradict his meaning. Her version of the meaning clearly relates to her need to be able to have friends. Jack's story asserts the primacy of the Mother–Child bond and the authority of the Father. Jo rejects this defiantly. Jack, it is clear, has a need to defend his own mother's behaviour (presumably in keeping *him* from his friends):

> 'That was a stupid mommy.'
> 'It was *not*,' he said with rare emphasis, and believed, from her expression, that she realized he was defending his own mother to her, or something as odd.

From this we can see that Jack identifies with the role of Roger Skunk. Updike's story ends with Jack's sense of alienation from his wife, Jo's Mommy. He seems to feel sympathy with the child's unhappiness and dislike of the mother's role (even though he himself was responsible for this version of the story). It is clear that Updike's tale invites a *psychological* interpretation. However, our analysis of narrative struc-ture has considerably assisted the process of interpretation by high-lighting the narrative processes involved in the psychological games people play.

The Russian Formalists distinguished between 'story' (the events in abstract) and 'plot' (the literary deployment of the events). Genette suggests a more subtle tripartite division: 'story' (*histoire*), 'text' (*récit*) and 'narration'. 'Text' is the written or spoken form of the events, while 'narration' is the mode of writing or speaking used in the 'text' (see 'Frontiers of Narrative' in *Figures of Literary Discourse*, 1982). Consider the 'narration' of the Updike tale. A common-sense response would be to say that Updike is the narrator, but this would be to ignore entirely the fictional construction of the tale which must include the construction of the narrator. Various attempts have been made to describe the links in the chain of narration from the author through to the reader. Here is a typical formulation:

Actual	– Implied	– Narrator –/–	Narratee –	Implied	– Actual
Author	Author			Reader	Reader

Structuralists exclude the actual author and reader from the textual level of a narrative. The sense of coherence or overall point of view we establish is not communicated directly to us by a narrative voice but is implied by a whole host of indirect signals. We call this coherence the 'implied author'. The term 'narrator' is reserved for the voice that communicates the story to us. The narrator can take many forms varying from a remote and godlike (omniscient) speaker to a totally unreliable and subjective speaker (see also section 3 on this). Updike's narrator is of the omniscient type; we are hardly aware of a narrator's presence. There are, however, a number of phrases which stand out as involving judgement or analysis which clearly do not emanate from Jack the fictional narrator of the Roger stories. Most of these phrases are related to the tale's psychological level:

> Jack continued with zest, remembering certain humiliations of his own childhood ... [he is telling Jo how the other animals shunned Roger Skunk]

> Jack didn't like women when they took anything for granted ... [Jo thinks he has finished the story]

It is true that one could imagine Jack consciously having these thoughts, but we are aware of the implied author's focusing of a psychological perspective in the narrator's dwelling on these thoughts. It is therefore possible to distinguish between:

1. Jack's thoughts.
2. The narrator's voice.
3. The implied author's perspective.

The structuralist term 'focaliser' is a helpful addition to our repertoire. It refers to the agent whose perceptions shape the presentation of what is said (not necessarily from the author's viewpoint). The focaliser can be internal or external to the story. Focalising is external in Updike's story. To put it into other terms, the implied author's external perspective is expressed through the impersonal narrator's voice.

What of the reader? The actual reader can, of course, be any type of person you could imagine, from the scarcely literate to the sophisticated critic. The 'narratee' is the reader as represented within the fiction. For example, a narrator may directly address the narratee ('My dear reader' or 'Dear Madam'). There is no narratee in Updike's tale. The 'implied reader', like the implied author, is a more subtle presence, and represents the sort of reader assumed by the text in various indirect ways. When Jack acts out the wizard's role he is startled by his daughter's 'rapt expression' which reminds him of 'his wife feigning pleasure at cocktail parties'. The narrator implies a certain sort of reader for whom feigning pleasure at cocktail parties makes sense as a social sign. Such a reader would know what cocktail parties are and would understand why it might be necessary to feign enjoyment at them. This may seem a rather obvious sort of assumption. However, by drawing attention to this 'implied reader' we begin to see just how much construction goes into fictional narrative.

The study of narrative theory shows the extent to which readers must unconsciously master a whole range of conventions (narrative structures) in order to process smoothly (at the level of common sense) the textual surface of a narrative fiction.

Section 9

Texts: Eugene O'Neill, *The Hairy Ape*, and Charles Dickens, *Great Expectations*
Theory: Metaphor and Metonymy

Readers commonly assume that prose is unadorned language, while poetry is deviant or ornamental language. They associate figures of speech with poetry rather than prose, even though they readily recognise that metaphors and other figures frequently occur in prose. They regard figurative language as essentially 'poetic' while prose, it is assumed, is functional and geared to reference. This view of language derives partly from scientific attitudes which encourage functional uses of language. In the early seventeenth century, Francis Bacon argued against 'copiousness' in scientific writings: if science is ever to give a practical and accurate account of the natural world, it must first purify its use of language, he argued, so that words can more accurately *reflect things*. Similarly, readers of classic novels tend to read them as if they were transparent windows looking out upon a real world beyond. The trouble with this surrender to realistic illusion is that it enforces a blindness to the linguistic mediation of narratives. Structuralists argue that language is always figurative, whether it is 'poetic' or 'prosaic'.

Roman Jakobson's essay on 'Two Types of Aphasia' is a seminal text in this tradition. He shows that all speakers and writers are biased towards one or other of two diametrically opposed linguistic predispositions. The two functions of *combination* and *selection* operate in language at every level. The first comes into play whenever we construct a sentence: we must link together a subject and predicate and must place any pronouns, nouns, epithets, adverbs, prepositions and conjunctions in their correct syntactical positions in the sentence to form a meaningful *sequence*. The second, selection, applies at every stage: any noun we introduce into a sentence is produced by a process of selection from the vast dictionary of language; any individual word implies a reject of its synonyms and antonyms. In the case of aphasics (those suffering speech defects), the loss of one dimension of linguistic organization produces a disabling bias in their speech. They function in only one of these dimensions: they can 'combine' or 'select' but not both. Jakobson went on to point out that the two disorders correspond to two figures of speech – metonymy and metaphor. Metonymy *deletes* certain elements in a sequence and treats part of a sequence (or context) as the whole (the crown = the monarch; the reds = communists). Metaphor uses the function of selection and involves the *substitution* of one element for a similar one from a different sequence or context. He also argued that in literary history certain literary movements were more inclined to privilege metonymy and others metaphor.

Jakobson's arguments challenge the 'Baconian' view of literary language. Prose fiction, for example, can no longer be regarded as broadly non-figurative. If some realistic fiction appears to avoid metaphor, it certainly does not avoid metonymy; the effect of realism involves the accumulation of details from a context which is 'represented' metonymicly by those details. Jakobson actually argued that while Romanticism was metaphoric, Realism was metonymic. Other critics, notably David Lodge, have shown that one cannot talk of an absolute division of the figures. However, the distinction is a useful one, and can be made to work in various ways and not necessarily in the ways suggested by Jakobson.

In Eugene O'Neill's stage directions to *The Hairy Ape* (1922) he signals clearly his intention of giving us a 'poetic' (metaphoric) rendering of the world:

> The treatment of this scene [1], or of any other scene in the play, should by no means be naturalistic. The effect sought after is a cramped space in the bowels of the ship, imprisoned by white steel. The lines of bunks, the uprights supporting them, cross each other like the steel framework of a cage. The ceiling crushes down upon the men's heads. They cannot stand upright. This accentuates the natural stooping posture which shovelling coal and the resultant over-development of back and shoulder muscles have given them. The men themselves should resemble those pictures in which the appearance of Neanderthal Man is guessed at. All are hairy-chested, with small, fierce, resentful eyes.
> (This and the following passage from *The Hairy Ape: The American Tradition in Literature*, vol. 2, ed. S. Bradley *et al.* (W. W. Norton, New York, 1967, pp. 1213, 1218))

The metaphoric bias is indicated in the title *The Hairy Ape*. The stokers on board the liner in the first scene are themselves ape-like, and the space in which they live and work is like a prison or a cage. The language of the play flows along the vertical line of *selection* and *substitution*: the context is not important and therefore the principle of combination is less significant. The parts of the work place are secondary to the parallel worlds from which metaphorical substitutions are drawn. Below decks is the 'bowels'; the steel *imprisons* and forms a 'cage'; the men's stooping posture makes them *resemble* Neanderthal Man and hairy apes. The central character, Yank, is like a wild ape in his violent hatred of the modern world to which he reacts by celebrating the violence which modern culture embodies in hellish machinery. The Irishman, Paddy, remembers the old days when work was more natural and more human:

> 'Twas them days men belonged to ships, not now. 'Twas them days a ship was part of the sea, and a man was part of a ship, and the sea joined all together and made it one. [*scornfully.*] Is it one wid this you'd be, Yank – black smoke from the funnels smudging the sea, smudging the decks – the bloody engines pounding and throbbing, and shaking – wid divil a sight of sun or a breath of clean air – choking our lungs wid coal dust – breaking our backs and hearts in the hell of the stokehole – feeding the bloody furnace – feeding our lives along wid the coal, I'm thinking – caged in by steel from a sight of the sky like bloody apes in the Zoo!

In 'realistic' prose a landscape is evoked by the combination of its elements and by the deletion of some in favour of others (we can never list all the elements in a context). Here the elements in Paddy's nostalgic seascape (men, sea, ships) lose their properties as individual parts of a whole: 'the sea joined all together and made it one'. This isn't metaphor, but it *is* a denial of metonymy. It makes for an idealised seascape not a realistic rendering. The passage moves steadily towards metaphoric substitution: the stokers' lives go into the furnaces along with the coal (lives = coal); the steel structures are cages; the men are apes in the Zoo. The elements of the context (the smoke, the dust, the furnace) are all reworked poetically: they cease to be primarily parts of a 'realistic' context and become parts of other (substituted) contexts (hell, zoo).

The play proceeds to develop its narrative line in terms of the initial metaphors established in Scene 1. The pale, white-clad Mildred, the empty product of capitalist wealth, is horrified when she sees the brutal Yank at work and sees him as a 'hairy ape'. He longs for revenge on her and all she stands for. Later in Manhattan, a lady's admiration for 'monkey fur' sends him into a fury: the fur is valuable but his own hairy ape skin is worthless in the eyes of the rich. He attacks a rich man and is thrown in prison: 'Steel. Dis is the Zoo, huh?' The other prisoners pick up the metaphor and extend it:

> VOICES [*With mocking laughter.*] You're in a cage aw right.
> A coop!
> A pen!
> A sty!
> A kennel!

This reminds one of Jakobson's observation that aphasics who lack the ability to form sequences speak often in short or 'one-word' sentences, providing mere substitutions for an initial term.

The play concludes with Yank's visit to an actual zoo and his death at the hands of a real hairy ape. He dies identifying himself as the original 'Hairy Ape'. The whole play moves along the metaphoric trajectory. There is, inevitably, some metonymic detail, but this is regularly subordinated to metaphor. This analysis confirms our subjective sense that the play is 'poetic' and not realistic.

Dickens' novels are exuberantly figurative and can be used to illustrate every conceivable use of metaphor and metonymy. In his work the two poles of figuration can swing across towards each other: metonymic detail becomes metaphoric, and *vice versa*. Metonymy is fundamental to Dickens' style in *Great Expectations*. The detailed characteristics of individuals and places are carefully sifted for representativeness. At the simplest level characters are defined visually by parts of them: Mr Wopsle is a Roman nose, a bald forehead and a deep voice; Old Barley is gout, rheum and growl. However, sometimes characteristics are context-bound. When Pip is at Miss Haversham's home, Satis, he is defined by his 'coarse hands' and 'common boots', while to Magwitch Pip is always a perfect gentleman. A physical context is important in the definition of character: Joe loses his sense of identity when he is away from the forge, the kitchen and the marshes. Of the many instances of Dickens' more complex interfusion of the two figures, consider this passage from chapter 26:

> It fell out as Wemmick had told me it would, that I had an early opportunity of comparing my guardian's establishment with that of his cashier and clerk. My guardian [the lawyer, Mr Jaggers] was in his room, washing his hands with his scented soap, when I went into the office from Walworth; and he called me to him, and gave me the invitation for myself and friends which Wemmick [Jagger's cashier and clerk] had prepared me to receive. 'No ceremony,' he stipulated, 'and no dinner dress, and say tomorrow.' I asked him where we should come to (for I had no idea where he lived), and I believe it was in his general objection to make anything

like an admission, that he replied, 'Come here, and I'll take you home
with me.' I embrace this opportunity of remarking that he washed his
clients off, as if he were a surgeon or a dentist. He had a closet in this
room, fitted up for the purpose, which smelt of the scented soap like a
perfumer's shop. It had an unusually large jack-towel on a roller inside the
door, and he would wash his hands, and wipe them and dry them all over
this towel, whenever he came in from a police-court or dismissed a client
from his room.

There are two figurative patterns discernible here. First, Jaggers is
defined metonymically in terms of his context and individual characteristics: his room, the closet, his scented soap, the jack-towel, his
economy with words, his lawyer's guardedness. A picture is rapidly
established through selective detail. However, one of the metonymic
fields – the one associated with towel and soap – is given an additional
(metaphoric) role. Pip, the narrator, actively intervenes to introduce
this figurative shift ('I embrace this opportunity of remarking'). Jaggers
'washed his clients off, as if he were a surgeon or a dentist'. Thus, the
actual context which generates a narrative sequence of a 'realistic' type
also generates a non-narrative metaphoric (poetic) level: Jaggers, the
lawyer, is like a surgeon or a dentist. The scented soap is not merely a
metonymic detail, evoking a 'real' setting, but a signifier in a metaphoric
substitution. Pip goes on to describe Jaggers emerging from a
particularly 'dark' case into his closet where he not only washed his
hands, but gargled, laved his face and 'took out his penknife and
scraped the case out of his nails'. The substitution of 'case' for 'dirt'
brings the two figures into witty conjunction.

A final example brings out the metonymic vitality of Dickens'
imagination. In this passage Pip thinks he is about to be murdered by
Orlick. He imagines Orlick hiding in the town as he had done after
murdering Pip's sister:

> My rapid mind pursued him to the town, made a picture of the street with
> him in it, and contrasted its lights and life with the lonely marsh and the
> white vapour creeping over it, into which I should have dissolved.
> It was not only that I could have summed up years and years and years
> while he said a dozen words, but what he did say presented pictures to me,
> and not mere words. In the excited and exalted state of my brain, I could
> not think of a place without seeing it, or of persons without seeing them.

The narrator's imagination is at one with Dickens'. With death
hanging over him his thoughts move dynamically and metonymically:
Orlick's words produce pictures of places and people – not just vague
thoughts about Orlick's character but the specific image of him in the

town and the contrasting image of the different landscape of the marsh (where Pip is trapped).

According to structuralist critics language does not 'refer' to 'things' (see section 10). Their theory undercuts the common-sense conception of prose fiction as a mirror-like 'representation' of a state of mind or of an imagined reality. Language cannot 'reflect', because signs do not simply correspond to things or to mental states. A piece of discourse always involves the play of relational systems of similarity and difference. The most fundamental structures of language are those which correlate to the vertical and horizontal poles of selection and combination. The figures of metaphor and metonymy constitute a fundamental binary opposition (see section 7) in the literary system. As the work of David Lodge has shown, Jakobson's discovery has proved a valuable aid in the analysis of literary texts of all kinds (see David Lodge, *The Modes of Modern Writing*, 1977).

There is apparently a danger that a structuralist position cuts off literature from its historical and social roots by denying it the power to represent an external reality. This is not necessarily the case. A literary sociology informed by structuralism recognises the 'textuality' of every discourse. That is, it sees that literature engages with 'society' not by directly reflecting upon the surface of its language a reality 'out there', but by re-presenting in different ways already existing systems of meaning. Jakobson's theory helps us to break down a false distinction between an opaque poetic language and a transparent prose language, and to see that all forms of language are figuratively constructed.

Chapter 4

Poststructuralism

Section 10

Text: Nathaniel Hawthorne, *The Scarlet Letter*
Theory: The Semiotics of the Sign and the Subject

The concept of the 'sign', first developed in the linguistic theory of Ferdinand de Saussure, has widely influenced modern literary theory. He argued that languages are sign systems (see *Course in General Linguistics*, 1974, part 2, chapter 4). The study of the nature of the linguistic sign ('semiotics') helps us to understand the structure of all (even non-linguistic) signs. A sign consists of two inseparable aspects – like two sides of a sheet of paper: an acoustic or graphic substance (meaningful sounds or marks), called the 'signifier', and a concept (what we 'think' when we produce or receive a signifier), called the 'signified'. Notice that Saussure does not include in the model of signification the *thing* or state of affairs corresponding to a signified. His linguistics does not attempt to include 'reference' in its picture of language. Signs work not by referring to things but by taking up a position within a system of signs. The lowest level of signification within the language system is the 'phoneme' (the smallest identifiable piece of sound). It is perfectly evident at this level that we identify a phoneme not as a piece of language which refers to something but as an element in a system of phonemes (see also section 7). We recognise /z/ because it can be compared and contrasted with /s/. Both phonemes are 'sybillants', but one is vocalised, the other is not. In the same fashion words come to have 'meaning' by functioning within a system of 'differences'. No word has meaning on its own: there is always present (invisibly, so to speak) in each word all the synonymous and antithetical terms in relation to which they are used by speakers.

Saussure also argued that the connection between a signifier and a signified is 'arbitrary': there is no natural connection between 'dog' and our mental image of a canine quadruped. This is common sense;

otherwise, we would have difficulty in explaining the existence of different languages. However, Saussure went on to say that once a connection is established between a signifier and a signified they form what is in practice a natural bond. We feel and behave as if the words we use are inseparable from the concepts we have of the things.

The intellectual movement known as structuralism was largely founded upon these assumptions. During the 1960s a number of theorists in psychology, philosophy, history and literary criticism used Saussure's theory of signs, but emphasised the unpredictable nature of their functioning. The writings of Jacques Derrida, Jacques Lacan, Michel Foucault and Roland Barthes are often called 'poststructuralist', although some prefer to regard them simply as later structuralists. In the work of many poststructuralists we begin to see a move towards what is sometimes called the 'rules of the signifier' – away from a stable linking of signifier and signified towards an instability which allows the signifier to call the tune. In Saussure's model, the arbitrary linking of signifier and signified is forgotten in the practice of actual speakers who behave as if a sign were a perfect unity, but in Lacan and others the signifier's arbitrariness determines the whole operation of signification. We may *think* that when we make an utterance we know what we are saying, and that our intention to mean something is the sole determinant of meaning. However, signifiers can never be fixed in that way. All utterances are capable of different interpretations, and the meaning we think we have intended and fixed may be undermined either by unconscious processes which operate at the level of the signifier (see section 11 on *Hamlet*), or by different interpretations which can be brought to bear on the signifiers we utter.

It is clear that the poststructuralists totally rejected the assumptions of traditional literary criticism. For them the authors of works had no power to control or fix their meanings. The origin of the work lay not in the mind of the author but in the entire complex network of significations from which the author produces a text. Barthes coined the phrase 'the death of the author' to describe the changed view of the text. In Barthes' *S/Z* the text is seen as a 'galaxy' of signifiers which the reader can open up in various ways by bringing into play the different critical languages which are available and none of which can 'close' the process of signification by imposing upon a signifier a final signified. The signifier will always remain free, always capable of being inter-woven with other signifiers from different discourses, to produce a different meaning. Barthes understandably tends to favour texts which allow the maximum possible freedom for the signifier and to disfavour those texts which try to limit its freedom. One further aspect of the signifier's rule must be explained before we examine a literary example. The linguist Emile Benveniste argued (in *Problems in General Linguistics*, 1971) that it is language which provides the possibility of subjectivity, because only language enables the speaker to situate himself or herself as an 'I' (the subject of a sentence). Jacques Lacan applies this theory to a child's psychological development. The signifiers 'I', 'male', 'son', for example, indicate a 'subject position' which a speaker must enter. This is not originally a biological necessity but a cultural process: we leave behind infantile stages of development and enter a social role which is only made possible by a complex process of repression and subjection. We become human 'subjects' by entering the positions which the signifier established in advance for us. However, our identity is never stable, because the relation between signifier ('I') and signified (the whole psychic process at work in me) is never fixed or final.

From a poststructuralist viewpoint Nathaniel Hawthorne's *The Scarlet Letter* (1849) is a compelling example. The novel actually seems to be about the devious processes of the signifier. The heroine Hester Prynne adopts the letter 'A' embroidered in scarlet on the front of her dress in penance for her adultery. She lives with her 'shame' in a New England community which is deeply imbued with Puritan values. Even though the letter is self-imposed (she accepts her punishment and does not leave the community), it is really Puritan ideology that fixes its meaning. The minister, Mr Dimmesdale, turns out to be the father of Hester's daughter Pearl, and at the end of the novel he confesses his sin publicly and dies. Hester's scarlet letter is the novel's central signifier: it weaves its ambiguous and haunting way through the text, scarcely allowing Hester to exist for a moment beyond its insistence. The letter seems to establish Hester's subject position irrevocably. The signified which Puritanism imposes upon the letter is 'adultery' together with all the connotations of shame and guilt that go with it. However, Hester's identity is not fixed by the signifier – she enters a subject-position which is always unstable despite the appalling power of Puritan ideology.

The struggle between Hester's subjection to the signifier's function in Puritan discourse and the (unconscious?) tendency for the signified to lose its anchorage in the signifier is often apparent. This slippage is perhaps caused by the effects of unconscious drives or simply 'desire'.

Unconscious desire inevitably rejects the repressive meanings of reason. These moments are not expressed in terms of open rejection of Puritan ideology. Sometimes Hester's attitude is ambiguous. For example, at one point in the woods Pearl asks her mother to tell her a story about 'the Black Man' of popular superstition who makes individuals write their names in his book in their own blood and sets his mark on their bosoms. She presses Hester to tell her whether the Black Man actually exists and whether the scarlet letter is his mark. She has been told that Hester meets the Man each midnight. Hester replies 'Once in my life I met the Black Man! [. . .] This scarlet letter is his mark!' Is Hester accepting and recognising the subject-position which the letter imposes on her? Is she accepting the Puritan version of her sin? Or is the Black Man simply Dimmesdale (in his black clerical garb), who laid his mark upon her (made love to her) 'Once' only? This second possibility suggests that Hester is placing the blame where it lies (though not overtly) and rejecting the Puritan sign.

Hester's daughter is somewhat tainted by her own sin according to the Puritans and is often alluded to as slightly demonic. When her mother, planning to escape with Dimmesdale, briefly throws off the sign of her shame, Pearl refuses to recognise her. The child points to the discarded letter:

> 'Bring it hither!' said Hester.
> 'Come thou and take it up!'
> 'Was ever such a child!' observed Hester aside to the minister. 'Oh, I have much to tell thee about her! But, in very truth, she is right as regards this hateful token. I must bear its torture yet a little longer – only a few days longer – until we shall have left this region, and look back hither as to a land which we have dreamed of. The forest cannot hide it! the mid-ocean shall take it from my hand, and swallow it up for ever!'
> With these words she advanced to the margin of the brook, took up the scarlet letter, and fastened it again into her bosom. [. . .]
> 'Dost thou know thy mother now, child?' asked she [. . .] 'Wilt thou come across the brook, and own thy mother, now that she has her shame upon her – now that she is sad?'
> 'Yes; now I will!' answered the child, bounding across the brook and clasping Hester in her arms. 'Now thou art my mother indeed! and I am thy little Pearl!' (chapter 19)
> (This and the following passages from *The Scarlet Letter and Selected Tales*, ed. T. C. Connolly (Penguin, Harmondsworth, 1970, pp. 124–5, 180, 227–8))

It is as if the letter has ceased to be exclusively bound to a Puritan meaning, and has come to signify simply 'mother'. For Pearl her mother's and her own identity are totally bound up with the scarlet letter. For her mother to cast off the letter would be to cast off her identity and thereby to obliterate Pearl's identity as her daughter. Once the scarlet letter has been readopted the mother/daughter subject-positions can be reassumed. It is clear from an earlier passage that Pearl's identity is indeed closely bound up with her mother's, not just as a daughter but as projection of the signifier of her mother's guilt. Hester dresses her young and beautiful child in a crimson velvet tunic embroidered with 'fantasies and flourishes of gold thread'. From a common-sense point of view Pearl's clothes are an emblem or expression of the sinful but joyous side of Hester. From a semiotic point of view, the 'insistence of the letter' (this is a phrase of Lacan's) is very prominent:

> But it was a remarkable attribute of this garb, and, indeed, of the child's whole appearance, that it irresistibly and inevitably reminded the beholder of the token which Hester Prynne was doomed to wear upon her bosom. It was the scarlet letter in another form: the scarlet letter endowed with life! The mother herself [. . .] had carefully wrought out the similitude, lavishing many hours of morbid ingenuity to create an analogy between the object of her affection and the emblem of her guilt and torture. But, in truth, Pearl was the one as well as the other; and only in consequence of that identity had Hester contrived so perfectly to represent the scarlet letter in her appearance. (chapter 7)

The signifier, the letter 'A', is repeated and continues to dominate the subject-positions of the characters throughout the novel. However, our sense of its inescapable meaning is often shaken. Even though the letter is almost constantly visible, the Puritan discourse which seems to fix its significance can never completely expel desire. The minister, who has repressed all visible symptoms of his part in the sin, is more deeply mastered by the Puritan discourse. He cannot escape the very signifier which Hester openly adopts. Several episodes in the novel allude to the secret presence of the letter on his breast. It is not clear whether this is real or imaginary. At the end of the novel the letter is seen by many imprinted on his flesh, but others insist it was not there. He is mastered by an invisible signifier.

What is made clear from a semiotic point of view is the doubleness of the whole process of the individual's identity. On the one hand our subject-positions are determined by the semiotic system, but on the other hand signification is always unstable. All attempts to impose meanings tend to produce unconscious resistance. However insistent the scarlet letter may be, its signified is never fixed or final. At various stages the letter is associated with signifieds which have no connection with adultery (for example, 'able', 'angel', 'Arthur', 'America', 'artist'). In times of trouble Hester takes on a new identity:

> there glimmered the embroidered letter, with comfort in its unearthly ray. Elsewhere the token of sin, it was the taper of the sick-chamber. [. . .] The letter was the symbol of her calling. Such helpfulness was found in her – so much power to do, and power to sympathize – that many people refused to interpret the scarlet A by its original signification. They said that it meant Able, so strong was Hester Prynne with a woman's strength. (chapter 13)

A fundamental principle of semiotics is the transferability of signifiers: a new context can allow a fresh connection between signifier and signified. The possibilities of interpretation are interminable: even a signifier of such awesome power can, in a new context, be assigned a new signified. This indicates that there is never any final Truth to be arrived at. We can never say that a particular signifier or string of signifiers (an entire literary work, for example) has been interpreted once and for all. To give it a final meaning (or to suppose that it has a final meaning) is merely to repress other possibilities of meaning. At one level we see Hester and Dimmesdale as subjected victims of a narrow and unyielding ideology; at another we see them as involved in an endless and complex process of unravelling and disconnecting the Scarlet Letter from its dominant signified.

Section 11

Text: William Shakespeare, *Hamlet*
Theory: Psychoanalytic Criticism

There have been numerous explanations of Hamlet's delay, many of which make some sense. For example, it can be argued that he has profound moral scruples about revenge which resemble the official Christian condemnation of it as an immoral act. Alternatively, it has been suggested that Hamlet has by nature a *reflective* disposition: he is inclined to *thought* rather than action. A third possibility is that he is *melancholy* by nature, suffers distracting thoughts of suicide and dark ideas of human wickedness, all of which disable him and prevent action. In this section I shall be examining psychological types of explanation.

Sigmund Freud believed that the myth of Oedipus expressed a profound insight into an important stage in the psychological development of human beings. He suggested that all sons go through a phase in their childhood when they desire to kill their fathers and marry their mothers. This desire is *unconscious* but none the less real in its effects. It marks an early stage in the child's development towards adult sexuality. Hitherto, the child, in the pre-Oedipal phase, has been oriented solely towards his mother. In the new phase, the father becomes 'rival' for his mother's affections. The threat of 'castration' forces the son to abandon his incestuous desire for his mother (all in the unconscious). The son now identifies with the father and perceives him as a role model rather than as a rival. In this way the transition to adult life and a mature male identity is achieved. However, as many of Freud's case studies show, the Oedipal phase is not completely surpassed, because the abandonment of mother love is achieved only by *repression* of unconscious desire. Repressed desires never go away: they remain latent, waiting for moments of crisis in the life of the adult. In other words, there is a price to pay for successful maturation. If the Oedipus Complex is not successfully overcome the son will preserve an unhealthy love for the mother and will find transition to heterosexual love difficult.

The relevance of Freud's theory of the Oedipus Complex to *Hamlet* is fairly obvious, and Freud himself was the first to point it out in 'Psychopathic Characters on the Stage' (*c*. 1905, *Art and Literature*, pp. 119–27). He argues that like all mature males Hamlet must have passed through the Oedipal phase and effectively repressed his Oedipal desires, but a crisis occurs in his life which brings the repressed desires to the surface again, totally disrupting Hamlet's ability to act. Hamlet is not aware of this damaging conflict inside himself, but he reveals its existence to the audience through certain symptoms in his behaviour and language. In his famous *Hamlet and Oedipus* (1949), Ernest Jones developed Freud's brief treatment of the play. Jones speculates that Hamlet had repressed his Oedipal feelings in adulthood so successfully that his admiration and love for his father were the most prominent of his filial emotions. Near the beginning of the play, Hamlet hears from the ghost the news that his father had been murdered. This realisation of his earliest childhood wish (to kill his father), which had been repressed so thoroughly, suddenly revives in him Oedipal 'thoughts' of incest and patricide. In his reading of the play Jones explains Hamlet's delay in psychological terms. Hamlet identifies himself with Claudius, because he did the thing which the son unconsciously desired to do. His guilty feelings (expressed by the ghost) move him to plan revenge on Claudius, but he desists because in killing Claudius he would be killing himself, since he too unconsciously wished to kill Old Hamlet. The speculations of Freud and Jones usefully highlight the psychodynamics of the drama, but lack textual focus. Is it possible to apply directly the concepts of psychoanalysis to the text itself?

The central feature of Hamlet's behaviour which requires explanation is his so-called 'madness'. The problem is that, even though he announces his intention (to Horatio) to assume 'an antic disposition', there are scenes in the play in which Hamlet appears to be genuinely deranged (especially in his interviews with Ophelia and during the grave-diggers' scene when he confronts Laertes). It may be impossible to determine whether Hamlet's derangement is genuine or not in some parts of the play. However, the question still arises – what sort of madness is it (whether assumed or real)? Any account of Hamlet's 'madness' which reduces his remarkable and unique patterns of discourse to a commonplace malady (melancholia) will lack conviction. One might add that it is not safe to treat Hamlet's presented behaviour as in some sense his native disposition. After all, he has immediate *reasons* to be melancholy and also explicitly tells us that he is intentionally going to behave oddly. We may still have to leave open the possibility that he actually becomes deranged at certain points in the play.

There is a further aspect of his words to Horatio (I.v) that deserves emphasis. He announces that he will talk in 'doubtful' phraseology and will be 'ambiguous'. This side of his 'madness' has little to do with 'melancholy'. As will be made clear later, the most recent kinds of psychoanalytic criticism treat the tricky and playful features of language as a guide to the slippery and unstable nature of personality. Shakespeare produced many other characters who are fond of ambiguity and 'equivocation'. The Elizabethan writers were generally addicted to word-play of all kinds. Modern readers are often less responsive to the pun and regard it as a low form of humour. Not so the Elizabethans, who relished a good pun. The word-play of Shakespeare's fools often takes the form of their misdirection of others' words to their own purposes. There is something subversive in this slippery use of language: it is often used to reveal truths which ordinary language refuses to recognise. Of all Shakespeare's characters Hamlet is the master 'equivocator'. He recognises its power when he complains of the gravedigger's use of it against him: 'We must speak by the card [*sc.*, unambiguously] or equivocation will undo us.' His own equivocations disturb, puzzle or irritate Gertrude, Claudius, Ophelia, Rosencrantz and Guildenstern. However, from a psychoanalytic viewpoint, we must add that Hamlet's word-play not only undermines the position of other people but, more importantly, it reveals Hamlet's own unconscious thoughts.

Polonius notes Hamlet's word-play and comments on the link between madness and cleverness with words: 'How pregnant sometimes his replies are – a happiness that often madness hits on.' However, Ophelia's madness, which drives her to harp on lost virginity and desertion, does not involve this cunning word-play. The Gentleman who reports to Gertrude Ophelia's distraction places a significant emphasis on her broken discourse:

> [She] spurns enviously at straws, speaks things in doubt
> That carry but half sense. Her speech is nothing,
> Yet the unshaped use of it doth move
> The hearers to collection. They aim at it,
> And botch the words up fit to their own thoughts,
> Which, as her winks and nods and gestures yield them,
> Indeed would make one think there might be thought,
> Though nothing sure . . . (IV.v.6–13)

The model of verbal communication described here is antithetical to Hamlet's. While he receives messages which he interprets and sends back transformed by equivocation, Ophelia's 'speech is nothing'. Her words lack coherence and require the listeners to piece them together to form meaningful utterances. Ophelia's speech demands that her listeners actively interpret it, while Hamlet's is a powerful interpretation of others' discourse. Her speech is full of gaps which require filling; Hamlet's speech multiplies meanings, and resembles what Roland Barthes called a 'writerly' text, which encourages a plurality of interpretations (see section 15). This polysemy is what makes it possible to decipher messages from Hamlet's unconscious mind.

The following exchange between Hamlet and Claudius shows how disruptive Hamlet's word-play can be:

> Claudius. How fares our cousin Hamlet?
> Hamlet. Excellent, i' faith, of the chameleon's dish. I eat the air, promise-crammed. You cannot feed capons so.
> Claudius. I have nothing with this answer, Hamlet. These words are not mine.
> Hamlet. No, nor mine now.
>
> (III.ii.92–6)

Hamlet suggests that the words one utters immediately cease to be one's own property. They can be wrenched from their original context or intention and be used for other purposes. This means that even though Hamlet's word-play gives him power over others, it is, in the end, not under his own control. A Freudian would say that when we make jokes or puns, and talk ambiguously, we are allowing unconscious thoughts to be expressed; we are permitting a temporary lifting of the censorship imposed by convention and by normal civilised restraints.

It has often been noticed that Hamlet seems to be obsessed by sex. His mother's incestuous marriage to Claudius enflames his disgust. Does Hamlet's word-play relate to the Oedipus Complex? Two early examples of equivocation centre on the question of kinship:

> Claudius. But now, my cousin Hamlet, and my son –
> Hamlet. A little more than kin, and less than kind.
>
> (I.ii.64–5)

Gertrude complains that he still seeks his 'noble father in the dust':

> Queen. Hamlet, thou hast thy father much offended.
> Hamlet. Mother, you have my father much offended.
> Queen. Come, come, you answer with an idle tongue.
>
> (III.iv.8–10)

Hamlet declares he cannot forget that she is 'your husband's brother's wife'. This harping on the disturbance in proper relations of kinship centres on *incest*. The sexual intercourse between a wife and her husband's brother could be regarded as incest in this period (Claudius refers openly to Gertrude as 'our sometime sister, now our queen'). Claudius is more than a mere kinsman ('cousin'); he has come uncomfortably close to Hamlet by marrying his mother, and yet is 'less than kind' (not his true father, with whom there would be the deep connections of family feeling). Hamlet's 'idle' (equivocal) tongue subversively identifies Old Hamlet and Claudius ('thy father'/'my father'), thus drawing attention to a difference, but also revealing the uncertainty of Hamlet's position as a gendered 'subject' (the term 'subject' is used in modern critical theory to mean the 'first person' – 'I'). Hamlet's whole identity as a male 'subject' depended on his successful repression of his childish Oedipal desires. This repression is now in the process of being lifted, with devastating results.

Hamlet's preoccupation with incest is related to his general obsessive concern with sexuality. Disgust at Gertrude's incestuous marriage drives him to see all sexuality as diseased and gross, and especially Ophelia's. Again his disgust is expressed in word-play: 'shall I lie in your lap? . . . Do you think I meant country [cunt-ry] matters?'

> *Hamlet.* That's a fair thought to lie between maid's legs.
> *Ophelia.* What is, my lord?
> *Hamlet.* Nothing.
>
> (III.ii.110–19)

Hamlet's strange word-play includes a dimension which is illuminated by psychoanalysis. As editors have pointed out 'nothing' can mean 'lack of the male "thing"', or the 'O' which lies between a maid's legs. A possibly related passage is the one in which Hamlet confuses Rosencrantz and Guildenstern with word-play. When asked where the body is (Polonius's) Hamlet replies 'The body is with the King, but the King is not with the body. The King is a thing –'. Guildenstern asks 'A thing, my lord?' Hamlet replies 'Of nothing' (IV.ii.26–9). Claudius has the male 'thing', which Hamlet would like to castrate and make a 'nothing'. Hamlet complains (III.iv.100, 103) to Gertrude that the King has pocketed 'the precious diadem' (taken the thing) and that he is 'A king of shreds and patches' (an image of castration) in contrast to the perfect image of the man that was his father.

Modern psychoanalytic criticism does not accept the way in which Freud and Jones treated characters as if they were real people. The only thing which psychoanalysis can examine according to the French theorist Jacques Lacan is 'textuality' itself – the discourse in which unconscious processes may be concealed. Lacan says that human subjects enter positions within a pre-established set of signifiers (mother – father – son – daughter) which can operate only within a language system. The libidinal drives (anal, oral and so on) of infanthood are brought gradually under the restraint of the Law of the Father, which is strongly connected with the entry into the symbolic system of language. However, the repressed desires never go away; their repression maintains a permanently 'split subject'. The unconscious processes are manifested only in dreams, jokes, slips of the tongue and so on. Lacan has argued, in his obscure but stimulating essay 'Desire and the Interpretation of Desire in *Hamlet*' (1977, 11–52), that Hamlet's word-play is profoundly significant for an understanding of the psychological dimension of the play:

> One of Hamlet's functions is to engage in constant punning, word play, double-entendre – to play on ambiguity. Note that Shakespeare gives an essential role in his plays to those characters that are called fools, court jesters whose position allows them to uncover the most hidden motives, the character traits that cannot be discussed frankly without violating the norms of proper conduct. It's not a matter of mere impudence and insults. What they say proceeds basically by way of ambiguity, of metaphor, puns, conceits, mannered speech – those substitutions of signifiers whose essential function I have been stressing. Those substitutions lend Shakespeare's theatre a style, a color, that is the basis of its psychological dimension. Well, Hamlet, in a certain sense must be considered one of these clowns.

The unconscious mind makes itself manifest only in distorted forms. Hamlet's repressed desires, too, come to the surface in this way. He himself states that he is aware of something going on in him which is more profound than his surface grief: 'But I have that within which passes show.' The externals of grief (black clothes, lamentation, tears) fail to 'denote' him (I.ii.83). The only things which truly denote him are 'signifiers' (the actual words he utters, divorced from any fixed meanings). Hamlet knows that his mother's early remarriage to her dead husband's brother is deeply disturbing and offensive, but 'that within' shakes him so deeply that even in soliloquies he cannot bring it fully to consciousness.

I have chosen to follow the Lacanian version of Freud's theory because it enables us to avoid speculating about Hamlet's family background or treating him as if he were a real person. We cannot ask

Hamlet to lie on the psychoanalyst's couch and tell us his problems. However, we *can* detect the symptoms of his psychological problems in the very words he utters in the play. Hamlet's word-play is the key to his unconscious. For a Lacanian, what is revealed by a study of his equivocations is the lurking trauma of the Oedipus Complex. This type of psychoanalytic criticism addresses the linguistic symptoms of unconscious processes, and is therefore in harmony with the *textual* focus of much contemporary literary criticism.

Section 12

Texts: William Wordsworth, 'Afterthought', and
Emily Dickinson, 'A Thought Went Up My Mind
Today'
Theory: Deconstruction

Modern critical theory often shatters common-sense attitudes towards
reading and interpretation. It is conventional to believe that a poem
should be treated as a direct utterance from a particular human
consciousness, that the poem's language can express the unique and
individual thought of that consciousness, that the poem's meaning is
determined by certain objective factors (the author's intention being
one), and that stable meaning is possible. These are, in essence,
metaphysical beliefs, which have links with other basic beliefs about
the nature of the world. Jacques Derrida's deconstructive readings are,
at one level, a remarkably far-reaching attempt to loosen the moorings
of virtually every intellectual tradition in Western thought (see
Positions, 1981, for a resumé of his theory). He accepts that we cannot
exist as social beings without some reliance on metaphysical commitments. However, he takes it upon himself to show how impossible it is for
us to escape the *differential* nature of language, or to extricate ourselves
from the 'aporias' of discourse (the 'undecidable' flow and counterflow
of all signification). It is not surprising that many literary critics have
been bitter in their criticisms of a form of analysis which leaves them
with no 'truth' and no determinate 'meaning'. This indeterminacy
affects the critic as much as the text. We cannot take up a neutral or
objective position from which to make a judgement or to settle the
meaning of the text. We, too, as speaking subjects are caught up in the
interminable weaving, unweaving and reweaving of the fabric of
discourse.
  There is no space in a brief account to explain the theoretical
ramifications of Derrida's thought, but a short summary of his characteristic 'method' (he never states it as such) is essential. Every piece of
discourse takes its bearings from the terms of a certain metaphysical

framework. The deconstructor begins by disclosing the hierarchically ordered, metaphysical substratum of a specific piece of discourse. The pairs of terms (soul/body, being/non-being, good/bad, content/form, truth/lies, essential/inessential, speech/writing, masculine/feminine and so on) are assumed to form a hierarchy of value or truth which allows the writer to exclude from the field of discourse those connotations or meanings which do not accord with the privileged terms. 'Body' is excluded as transitory and inessential; 'form' is superficial and variable; 'feminine' is a defective or weaker form of 'masculine'. The deconstructor proceeds by reversing the hierarchy, not perversely but by discerning a chink in the discourse which allows this reversal. Finally, the newly-asserted hierarchy is itself displaced and is not allowed to install a new 'truth' or structural fixity. The rule of indeterminacy prevails. While structuralists had treated binary oppositions (see section 7) as stable terms in a formal structure, Derrida sees them as organised in unstable disequilibrium.

This brief formulation of Derridean deconstructive reading ideally requires a very much longer theoretical exposition, but on the other hand it is more in the spirit of Derrida simply to offer a deconstructive reading. A truly deconstructive critical practice would allow the play of discourse to work through its own writing, throwing into question its own truth. In a sense any *demonstration* of Derridean 'method' is totally un-Derridean in spirit. In practice, the exigencies of explanation require this un-self-deconstructive approach to the topic of deconstruction. This warning is necessary, since we cannot adopt a Derridean theory without radically modifying critical practice.

Consider William Wordsworth's poem 'Afterthought':

> I thought of thee [the river Duddon], my partner and my guide,
> As being passed away. – Vain sympathies!
> For, backward, Duddon! as I cast my eyes,
> I see what was, and is, and will abide;
> Still glides the Stream, and shall forever glide;
> The Form remains, the Function never dies;
> While we, the brave, the mighty, and the wise,
> We Men, who in our morn of youth defied
> The elements, must vanish – be it so!
> Enough, if something from our hands have power
> To live, and act, and serve the future hour;
> And if, as toward the silent tomb we go,
> Through love, through hope, and faith's transcendant dower,
> We feel that we are greater than we know.
> (From *The Poetical Works*, ed. E. de Selincourt (Oxford University Press, London, New York and Toronto, 1936, p. 303))

We may summarise the poem's thought in a series of points:

1. The river appeared to be transient.
2. The river is in fact eternal.
3. Content and appearance change, but Form and Function remain the same.
4. We men are transient.
5. There are two consolations:
   (a) Our art ('something from our hands') will survive us;
   (b) Faith, hope and charity tell us that there is more to us than we can know rationally.

The metaphysical hierarchies operating in the poem are: permanence/transience, form/content and function/existence. The first term in each case is valued above the second. Transience is loss: the memory of Duddon is of a river that has 'passed away'. The *true* Duddon is eternal. The true Duddon is something like a Platonic Idea (Plato's Idea is sometimes called 'Form') which is the permanent mental essence of something (bedness, for example, the common essence of all beds). The forms and functions of things in this sense never change. Wordsworth's initial privileging of 'form' over 'content' actually reverses the more usual (to us) prioritising of 'content' over 'form'. Often we treat 'form' as a mere external garment overlaying a more substantial content. We may think of a poem's 'content' as being more important than its 'form'. Wordsworth adopts the typically Romantic construction of the opposition: 'form' is essential and unchanging, while 'content' is disposable and transient. However, the parallel human dichotomy (men/art) is of a different order: what survives is 'something from our hands' – something we make (a poem, a painting, a cathedral). Just as the river will always provide a beauty and a purpose for the future, so men's artifacts will survive them and serve the artistic and moral purposes of future generations. The history of the term 'form' is itself sufficiently 'undecidable' to open the possibility of deconstruction. In the Platonic tradition, reworked in the poem, 'form' is superior to content: all particular beds are derived from the 'form'. Literary critical usage sometimes follows this traditional valuation: poetic achievement is formal, while the 'content' of a poem is secondary. However, others prioritise 'content' and regard literary form as merely an empty vessel in which the substance of the poem is placed.

The weight of Wordsworth's endorsement of permanence is felt in the final invocation of love, hope and faith. As is common in Wordsworth's poetry, terms which carry Christian connotations take on the metaphysical depth of religion without being explicitly religious. This dimension reinforces the privileging of permanence. What the artist makes shares something of the eternity of the Christian afterlife. However, the precariousness of the insight is marked in the poem's title – 'Afterthought'. The first thought (of transience) is corrected by a second, later (and perhaps chance) thought. We are almost invited to reverse the hierarchy: what we create, though it may outlast us, is also transient. To 'serve the future hour' involves performing *another* purpose, which takes on a *different* meaning or function for a different age. The 'form' and 'function' of Wordsworth's poems will be determined by the way they are read by later generations. All that will survive is an *empty* form and not an eternal Platonic Form. The feeling of greatness which inspires the artist is entirely a matter of 'faith' after all. In reality they go 'toward the silent tomb' with no certainty that their work can 'live and act' in the future except as an empty set of signifiers awaiting the interpretive power of a new reader. This reversal of the hierarchy cannot be allowed to remain in force as a new 'violent' hierarchy. The famous saying of the Greek Presocratic philosopher Heraclitus ('everything flows') stressed transience, but, as Wordsworth sees, there can also be a permanence in the flowing as well as a transience. It is worth noting that, while a New Critical reading of the poem would see this ambivalence as evidence of Wordsworth's unified sensibility and his balanced vision of truth, a deconstructive reading of the poem leaves the question of 'truth' open. A further question remains unanswerable: is the poem itself a proof of Wordsworth's survival or his passing away? When we read, do we read the same poem or produce another poem? The play of '*différance*' (see below) makes this question as unanswerable as the others.

The American disciples of Derrida (they include Geoffrey Hartman, Paul de Man, and J. Hillis Miller) have developed versions of deconstruction adapted to literary criticism and especially to the tradition of American New Criticism. De Man's writings, for example, often suggest that the literary text knows itself, is aware, so to speak, of its own strategies, and that it is self-deconstructing. The following reading of a poem by Emily Dickinson does not follow de Man's actual approach but attempts to show in what ways a poem can be said to be self-deconstructing. This poem, like Wordsworth's, is concerned with a thought:

A thought went up my mind today
That I have had before,

But did not finish, – some way back,
I could not fix the year,

Nor where it went, nor why it came
The second time to me,
Nor definitely what it was,
Have I the art to say.

But somewhere in my soul, I know
I've met the thing before;
It just reminded me – 'twas all –
And came my way no more.
(From *The Complete Poems*, ed. T. H. Johnson (Faber and Faber,
London, 1975, p. 345))

In philosophical terms it is immediately apparent that this poem is less metaphysically confident than Wordsworth's: the status of the 'thought' is highly problematic, and its origin and meaning are indeterminate. 'Went up' emphasises the thought's *otherness*: the form of the verb suggests an unknown traveller walking up the mind's driveway. The metaphysical question raised by the poem concerns Being and Non-being. Does the thought have being? After all, it is a 'thing'. On the other hand, its origin, destination, meaning, nature and very existence are in doubt. A conventional reading would probably naturalise the poem by reducing it to a commonplace idea: we sometimes experience a *déja vu*, a sense of having had the same experience twice. Further, some thoughts we have are not expressible in words. However, these paraphrases do no justice to the poem's indeterminacy. What is in doubt is the very *presence* of the thought.

According to Derrida, Western metaphysics treats the spoken word as the incarnation of a thought: the word represents the thought and contains its full 'presence'. From a deconstructive point of view language has no ability to represent thought in this way; all discourse is subject to the play of *'différance'*. The word includes the meanings 'to differ', 'to disperse', and to 'defer'. Signifiers (spoken or written words) can never have settled signifieds (concepts of things); language cannot capture 'presence'. Language is a system of 'differences' and not a collection of units of meaning. Signifiers 'disperse' meaning and 'defer' presence.

Something of this deferral of presence is suggested in the poem. There is a sense that Non-being and Being are one, that the thought, though non-existent (unfinished and unlocatable), has the force of a 'thing'. This 'thing' is really no-thing. That there is something is determined only by the repetition (it comes again). Its return is not to be repeated, but marks its existence. Once might be a dream, but twice makes it a 'thing'. The normal use of 'reminded' is travestied here: the 'thing' entered the mind twice in some unlocated part of the soul. To be re-minded of the same non-thought is to attribute Being to Non-being. The poem is aware, so to speak, of the undecidable question of Being and Non-being: it deconstructs itself by forestalling any movement towards a definite hierarchy of terms. The poem, like a deconstructive reading of it, seems to block any movement towards determinate meaning. It has no centre, no term which supports a settled structure. Its discourse is 'aporetic' – relentlessly indeterminate.

The challenge which this type of theory produces is especially disturbing, because the concepts of 'indeterminacy' and '*différance*' erode all notions of knowledge, objectivity, identity and historical truth. Some critics (Marxists and feminists, for example), in pursuit of moral and political commitments, have used deconstructive concepts in order to disrupt other people's discourses and forms of knowledge. That is to say, it is possible to use Derrida's tactics for particular ideological purposes without being committed to the strictly textual and playful practices of American deconstructive critics. Unless we are prepared to use deconstruction politically – as a way of overcoming repressive discourses – we will be driven to accept a sterile formalism. I myself reject the idea that deconstruction simply affirms the 'free play' of the world, and requires that we lose ourselves in the endless and interminable aporias of signification.

Section 13

Text: William Shakespeare, *Measure for Measure*
Theory: New Historicism

Throughout the nineteenth century there ran side by side two contradictory approaches to the study of literary history. One presented the history of literature as a series of isolated monuments, achievements of individual genius. The other was 'historicist', and saw it as part of a larger cultural movement. The latter was often influenced either by Hegelian idealism, or, later, by the evolutionary naturalism of Herbert Spencer. The rise of 'historicism' led to the publication of several major books which studied literature in the context of social, political and cultural history. Historicism understood literary history as a developing totality which reflects a nation's evolving spirit. Thomas Carlyle expressed the characteristic historicist attitude when he wrote: 'The history of a nation's poetry is the essence of its history, political, scientific, religious.' (*Edinburgh Review*, 53, no. 105, 1831)

In the twentieth century E. M. W. Tillyard wrote an extremely influential historicist account of the culture of Shakespeare's period – *The Elizabethan World Picture* (1943). He argued, in Hegelian fashion, that the literature of the period expressed a common spirit of the age, which centred on ideas of divine order, the chain of being and the correspondences between earthly and heavenly existences. For Tillyard, Elizabethan culture is a seamlessly unified system of meanings, which could not be disturbed by unorthodox or dissenting voices. He believed that the Elizabethans regarded 'disorder' as outside the norm, and that deviant figures such as Marlowe never seriously challenged the settled world-view of the age.

New Historicists, whose work has been profoundly influenced by Michel Foucault and other poststructuralist thinkers, remain within the old historicism in the sense that, like Tillyard, they are interested in grasping the interconnections between literature and the larger culture. However, in every other respect they depart from Tillyard's approach.

The poststructuralist intellectual revolution of the 1960s and 1970s challenges the older historicism on several grounds:

1. There are two meanings of the word 'history': (a) 'the events of the past' and (b) 'telling a story about the events of the past'. Poststructuralist thought makes it clear that history is always 'narrated', and therefore the first sense is untenable. The past can never be available to us in pure form, but always in the form of 'representations'.

2. Historical periods are no longer conceived as unified entities. There is no single 'history', only discontinuous and contradictory 'histories'. There was no single Elizabethan world-view. The idea of a uniform and harmonious culture is a myth imposed on history and propagated by the ruling classes in their own interests.

3. Historians can no longer claim that their study of the past is detached and objective. We can never transcend our own historical situation. The past is not something which confronts us as if it were a physical object, but is something we construct from already written texts of all kinds which we construe in line with our particular historical concerns.

4. The relation between literature and history must be rethought. There is no stable and fixed 'history' which can be treated as the 'background' against which literature can be foregrounded. All history (histories) is 'foreground'. 'History' is always a matter of telling a story about the past, using other texts as our intertexts. Literary works should no longer be treated as sublime and transcendent expressions of the 'human spirit' but as texts among other texts.

The New Historicists in America and their counterparts, the 'cultural materialists' in Britain, have produced a substantial body of work on Renaissance literature and society. The two key influences on their work are Michel Foucault and Louis Althusser. For both, human life is shaped by social institutions and specifically by ideological discourses. Both conceive ideology as actively constituted through social struggle, and both show how at another level dominant ideologies sustain and keep social divisions in place. Althusser's theory (see section 22) abandons the orthodox interpretation of ideology as 'false consciousness' in favour of a theory which (1) situates ideology firmly within material institutions (political, juridical, educational, religious and so on), and (2) conceives ideology as a body of discursive practices which, when dominant, sustain individuals in their places as 'subjects'

(subjects them). Every individual is 'interpellated' (or 'hailed') as a subject by a number of ideological discourses, which together serve the interests of the ruling classes. Foucault also emphasises that discourses are always rooted in social institutions. He shows that social and political power works through discourse. For example, certain dichotomies are imposed as definitive of human existence and are operated in ways which have direct effects on society's organisation. Discourses are produced which use concepts of madness, criminality, sexual abnormality and so on, defined in relation to concepts of sanity, justice and sexual normality. These discourses have no universal validity but are merely historically dominant ways of controlling and preserving social relations of exploitation.

How do these ideas operate in Renaissance literary criticism? The New Historicists, Stephen Greenblatt, Louis Montrose and Jonathan Goldberg, explore the ways in which Elizabethan literature (especially drama, masque and pastoral) act out the concerns of the Tudor monarchy, reproducing and renewing the powerful discourses which sustain the system. While some Americans have dissented from this rather functionalist view, it must be said that American New Historicism has been associated with a pessimistic understanding of discursive power in literary representations of the Elizabethan and Jacobean social order. While many of Shakespeare's plays give voice to subversive ideas, such questionings of the prevalent social order, they suggest, are always 'contained' within the terms of the discourses which are set in play. Greenblatt often thinks of subversion as an expression of an inward necessity: we define our identities always in relation to what we are not, and therefore what we are not must be demonised and objectified as the 'other'. The mad, the unruly and the alien are internalised 'others' which help us to consolidate our identities: their existence is allowed only as evidence of the rightness of established power. British 'cultural materialists', influenced by Althusser (see section 22) and Mikhail Bakhtin (see section 24), have developed a less pessimistic and more politically radical type of historicism. Jonathan Dollimore and others have adopted some of the theoretical refinements to be found in Raymond Williams' *Marxism and Literature*, especially his distinction between 'residual', 'dominant' and 'emergent' aspects of culture. By replacing the Tillyardian concept of a single spirit of the age with Williams' more dynamic model of culture, the materialists have freed a space for the exploration of the full structural complexity of Renaissance society including its subversive and marginalised elements. A further important concern of Dollimore and others is with the 'appropriations' of cultural representations which occurred at the time and subsequently. The meanings of literary texts are never entirely fixed by some universal criterion, but are always in play, and subject to specific (often politically radical) appropriations, including those of cultural materialists themselves.

Shakespeare's *Measure for Measure* was first performed during 1604 in the second year of James I's reign and not long after the theatres were reopened following the plague. There are a number of possible links between Vincentio, the Duke, and James, but, from a New Historicist viewpoint, the most important one is the shared concern with authority. The play dramatises the tensions and contradictions inherent in the discourses of Tudor–Stuart monarchic power. The 'other' in this instance is the urban underworld, which is regarded as a threat to order. Lucio, a smart man about town, is genuinely subversive; he slanders the Duke, and momentarily undermines his authority. The Duke admits that he has allowed the law to lose its terror: 'Liberty plucks Justice by the nose' (I.iii.28). Authority needs to maintain a delicate balance between terror and justice. Terror can retain its power provided that the alternations of punishment and mercy preserve a deterrent uncertainty. Having allowed the 'rod' to become 'mock'd', the Duke, who doubts his own capacity to preserve the balance, relies on Angelo to re-establish his authority. Angelo enforces the laws ruthlessly and, as it turns out, hypocritically.

Authority is asserted against one form of transgression in particular – sexual liberty. As Jonathan Dollimore argues in his essay on the play (in *Political Shakespeare*, 1985), the anxiety of rulers and their need to legitimise their authority leads them to cast out specific 'others'. Using already constructed dichotomies which establish the deviance of certain classes and groups, authority is able to use them at moments of crisis to bolster itself. The play's opening clearly represents such a moment of crisis during a period of war and plague. The demonisation of sexual deviance is the instrument by which those in authority reassert the relations of power.

The central means available to reproduce relations of power is ideology itself. In this play religion is an important site of ideological power. And yet, interestingly, the play also shows the instability of religious interpellations and the unceasing need to re-establish authority. Claudio, who is condemned to death by Angelo for getting Juliet with child, is visited by the Duke (disguised as a friar) and persuaded to 'be absolute for death'. The Duke's speech on death draws upon Christian and stoic philosophy, and aims to situate Claudio in a subject position which will help him to conform to the will of the law. Even earlier in the play Claudius had completely accepted the divine sanctioning of earthly justice ('the demi-god, Authority') which defines human nature and the permissible limits of human action. However, after his sister Isabella's visit Claudio relapses ('Death is a fearful thing'), and rebels against religious injunctions. In a different way, Barnadine, an avowed murderer, shows the possibility of a total recalcitrance towards authority: the Duke is completely unable to settle his mind for death ('A creature unprepar'd, unmeet for death'). From a New Historicist viewpoint these resistances and lapses are an important indicator of the instability of all ideological discourses. However, some New Historicists (Greenblatt, for example) would argue that the resistances are pre-scripted by the dominant discourse, and that the demonisation of a Barnadine secures the authority of the law to define arbitrarily what is acceptable, normal and legitimate.

Many of the play's contradictions centre on Angelo. Does the Duke place him in authority knowing him to be a hypocrite ('Hence shall we see/If power change purpose, what our seemers be')? Or does he use him because he thinks Angelo's severity will purge society of its corruption? A further contradiction lies in Angelo's relationship to justice. On the one hand, he sees himself as the impersonal instrument of the 'law' ('It is the law, not I, condemn your brother'); on the other hand, he is guilty of the most flagrant manipulation of the law to serve his own lust. For a New Historicist, Angelo's desire is not a mere personal lapse, but is already part of the authoritarian discourse of the law. The very violence of Angelo's suppression of desire (in himself and others) indicates the strength of its presence. Isabella's first interview with Angelo in which she sues for her brother's life contains precisely this discursive pattern:

> *Angelo.* Why do you put these sayings upon me?
> *Isabella.* Because authority, though it err like others,
>   Hath yet a kind of medicine in itself
>   That skins the vice o' th' top. Go to your bosom,
>   Knock there, and ask your heart what it doth know
>   That's like my brother's fault. If it confess
>   A natural guiltiness, such as is his,
>   Let it not sound a thought upon your tongue
>   Against my brother's life.
> *Angelo.* *[aside]* She speaks, and 'tis such sense
>   That my sense breeds with it.

(II.ii.134–43)

Isabella shows that authority is blind to its own complicity with the very transgression it impugns. She also sees that this complicity actually makes for a more punitive application of the law. Angelo's aside confirms the entire analysis. The pun on 'sense' is especially apt, since it draws attention to the law's internalisation of its 'other'. Isabella's purity and rationality *produces* Angelo's desire: her 'sense' (reason) breeds his 'sense' (desire). Indeed her speech actually refers to this desire lurking at the heart of all authority. Later she puts her finger precisely on the pernicious dialectic of authority, whose agents bid 'the law make curtsey to their will,/Hooking both right and wrong to th' appetite,/To follow as it draws' (II.iv.174–6).

By using the New Historicist method of reading we gain a sense of the play's exploration of the power of legal and religious discourses as they work to sustain the social order. We also see the possibility of resistances and transgression, though some have argued that the dominant discourses always *produce* resistance only to *contain* it, and thus preserve themselves.

Chapter 5

Reader-response Criticism

Section 14

Text: William Wordsworth, 'To H.C., Six Years Old'

Theories: Phenomenology (Geneva School of Critics), and Deconstruction

Before considering specifically reader-oriented theories, I would like to discuss an influential school of criticism which searches for the distinctive types of consciousness which structure particular writers' works. The Geneva critics believed that it is possible to experience and describe a writer's way of seeing the world. After giving a phenomenological reading of a poem by Wordsworth I shall offer some criticisms of the theory, and contrast the reading with a deconstruction of the poem (on deconstruction see also sections 12 and 15).

The term 'phenomenology' means the 'study of phenomena', and the Greek word 'phenomenon' means 'that which appears'. Edmund Husserl, the father of modern phenomenology, asserts that the only thing we can be certain of is our own consciousness of the world. We cannot say with any philosophical certitude that objects exist 'out there' outside our minds, but we *can* say that objects *appear* to our consciousness. He argues that consciousness of the world is not a passive accepting of the existence of things (like a mirror reflecting objects) but rather an active *forming* and *intending* of the world. All objects are 'intentional objects'. This may seem a very subjective and precarious view of reality, but in fact Husserl regards the individual consciousness as the sole source of our understanding of the world. Further, we are not limited to a mere chaotic flux of experience (images flashing through our minds like light through a window) but we can grasp in our consciousness the essential features of things. We come to know these 'essences' only through our mental processes of reflection: we discover what is permanent in an object and what gives it its individual being as that particular object.

The so-called Geneva School of critics, which included the Swiss writers Jean Rousset and Jean Starobinski, the Frenchman Jean-Pierre

Richard, and the American J. Hillis Miller, applied Husserl's form of phenomenology to literary criticism. What was the result? First, they treated the literary text as the site of an authentic consciousness. A poem expresses the way a writer subjectively experiences the world as an object of consciousness. Everything outside the poem is 'bracketed out'. What matters is the *state of consciousness* embodied in it, not the things to which it could be related.

The Belgian critic Georges Poulet provides a very lucid formulation of this critical approach in his well-known essay 'Criticism and the Experience of Interiority' (in *The Structuralist Controversy*, 1972). He argues that, unlike a vase or even a statue, a book does not present itself primarily as an exterior object, but comes across as transferring to the reader an 'interiority'; a book is the container of a consciousness. A book involves the coming together of two consciousnesses – the writer's and the reader's. Poulet sees this as a strange and teasing actuality: *the reader is made to think the thoughts of another.* The book I read lives its life through me like a vampire living off another's blood. When I read I have direct access to the author's ideas, feelings and 'modes of dreaming and living', and also I myself actually think these thoughts as I read. However, it is important to emphasise that the other 'I' which inhabits the texts and lives in me when I read is not simply the real author but the *consciousness* which is embodied in the work. My access to this other consciousness is only through the work. Poulet also believes that my acquaintance with the various writings of an author will give me access to the author's structure of identity – the author's 'common essence' – which is something h..rd to define except in very abstract terms. It is the very shape of the author's mental universe.

Wordsworth's 'To H.C. Six Years Old', a poem addressed to the son of Samuel Taylor Coleridge (poet, philosopher and Wordsworth's friend and collaborator), compels the reader to live a particularly intense and complex life of the mind. The poem is very overtly what the speaker *thinks* about the child; the 'I' of the poem thinks its object (the child) in a very distinctive manner. How could we characterise the essence of this 'I' – the structure of consciousness which the poem expresses? Here is the poem:

> O Thou! whose fancies from afar are brought;
> Who of thy words dost make a mock apparel,
> And fittest to unutterable thought
> The breeze-like motion and the self-born carol;
> Thou Faery Voyager! that dost float
> In such clear water, that thy Boat

May rather seem
To brood on air than on an earthly stream;
Suspended in a stream as clear as sky,
Where earth and heaven do make one imagery;
O blessed Vision! happy Child!
That art so exquisitely wild,
I think of thee with many fears
For what may be thy lot in future years.

I thought of times when Pain might be thy guest,
Lord of thy house and hospitality;
And grief, uneasy Lover! never rest
But when she sate within the touch of thee.
Oh! too industrious folly!
Oh! vain and causeless melancholy!
Nature will either end thee quite;
Or, lengthening out thy season of delight,
Preserve for thee, by individual right,
A young Lamb's heart among the full-grown flocks.
What hast thou to do with sorrow,
Or the injuries of tomorrow?
Thou art a dew-drop, which the morn brings forth,
Not doom'd to jostle with unkindly shocks;
Or to be trail'd along the soiling earth;
A Gem that glitters while it lives,
And no forewarning gives;
But, at the touch of wrong, without a strife
Slips in a moment out of life.
(From *The Poetical Works*, ed. E. de Selincourt (Oxford University Press,
London, New York and Toronto, 1936, p. 70))

The poem is structured throughout by an underlying *dualism* of thought
which moves between the timeless and the temporal. The speaker (the
poet, it seems) holds the object of his thought in a dynamic tension
between the poles of dualistic vision. He moves between the ideal and
the real, the heavenly and the earthly, the timeless and the temporal.
It is the last of these dichotomies which is essential: it is time which
seems to threaten the child's perfection and bring upon him the threat of
changes. Here is a tabulation of the two poles as presented in the poem:

unutterable thought	Pain/grief
Faery Voyager	injuries of tomorrow
air	earthly
Vision	the soiling earth
Lamb's heart	full-grown flocks

On the left are the attributes of the child's ideal existence as a perfect being; on the right the imperfections which threaten that existence. The ideal attributes are all aspects of the timeless condition of the child's perfection, the negative attributes all aspects of temporal existence and change. When the poet has established the visionary child he shifts gear for a moment by introducing a *thought* ('I think') of the future ('what may be thy lot in future years'). Even the odd transition in the second part of the poem to a past tense ('I thought') points towards this preoccupation with time (present – past). The solution to the dilemma is to override the whole temporal dimension – to speak as if time does not exist: such is the child's ideal existence that he will either disappear completely from the temporal world (note that the poet does not say 'die', which is a temporal concept) or nature will lengthen out the child's 'season of delight' so that the depredations of time can be evaded. The image of the dew-drop echoes a poem of that name by the seventeenth-century poet Andrew Marvell, who treats the dew-drop as an emblem of the soul which rejoins heaven (as the dew does by evaporation!). Wordsworth's dew-drop is called a 'gem', a description which in one sense contradicts the essentially fragile nature of dew. The image brings us back to the child's unchanging and eternal perfection. The dew and child will slip 'in a moment out of life'; the phrase could carry 'earthly' (temporal) connotations of dying or dissolving into nothing, but once again the avoidance of reference to death must be noted. 'Slips in a moment out of life' suggests the soul's *retreat* from the soiling touch of earth. This means that 'while it lives' should be glossed as 'while it has an earthly existence'. From a phenomenological viewpoint the entire poem is a consistent vision based on a particular structure of consciousness which shapes experience from beginning to end.

A well-informed reader might object to this procedure, arguing that the type of consciousness discovered by the phenomenological critic is quite obviously related to what is usually called Neo-Platonism. The poet refers to those 'fancies' which are brought 'from afar'. The Neo-Platonist, too, believes that human souls had an ideal pre-existence and bring this perfection with them to their earthly conditions; the imperfections of earthly existence include those of matter and time, which involve change and degrade the perfect substance of eternal Being. Wouldn't it be simpler to say that Wordsworth is writing a Neo-Platonic poem (the same could be said of his 'Ode: Intimations of Immortality')? Leaving aside the subtle nuances of Wordsworth's thought, we have to say that phenomenological critics are concerned only with the structure of consciousness which is manifested directly in the literary work. The similarities between one structure and another are quite beside the point, they would argue. Other objections to Poulet's theory of reading can be made. From a poststructuralist perspective his approach is essentialist: even though he distinguishes between a biographical author and a textual consciousness, he still assumes the existence of an essential mental set – a structure of consciousness. He presupposes too a unity of consciousness across a writer's entire *oeuvre*, ignoring the shifts, contradictions and breaks which can occur between phases of a writer's productions and even within individual texts. Poulet, in short, preserves a link with romantic notions of spiritual and imaginative unity.

A deconstructive reading of the poem would start with a similar move – the identification of the governing conceptual dichotomy, which Derrida calls a 'violent hierarchy'. As the term suggests, deconstruction does not start by assuming that the poem has a harmonious equilibrium. More fundamentally the deconstructive critic denies the very concept of 'consciousness' as some sort of unique and individual awareness. In the structuralist tradition (from which Derrida's thought derives) 'textuality' is more fundamental than consciousness. In a sense consciousness is produced by textuality. The way we shape the world in thought is determined by a pre-existing system of 'differences' which operates through language. Wordsworth's poem takes up the dualistic pattern which runs through Neo-Platonic thought and *privileges* one of its terms. If we glance back at our two columns of phrases we can see that the first column is privileged at the expense of the second. In other words, the poet's ordering of experience is determined by the hierarchy of terms. However, the deconstructive critic does not leave the analysis at this level, but proceeds to show that the privileging of one set of terms is not stable. We can unpick the apparently settled threads of the poem and reverse the hierarchy by saying that in fact time is the privileged term. It is the sheer power of time and its accompanying changes which forces the poet to imagine the child slipping out of life, and compels him to suspend reason in supposing that the child's ideal existence could be 'lengthened out'.

If we look more closely at the poem's discursive surface we may notice that there are even signs of self-deconstruction. For example, consider the following passage:

> thy Boat
> May rather seem
> To brood on air than on an earthly stream;
> Suspended in a stream as clear as sky,
> Where earth and heaven do make one imagery;

The stream in which the child's metaphorical boat glides appears to be in the sky rather than on the earth. This opposition between air and earth seems at first to support the dichotomies timeless/temporal and ideal/real. However, this is contradicted in the next phrases which present the fusion of the ideal and the real ('heaven and earth do make one imagery'). Suddenly, the dichotomies and their attendant hierarchisation is dissolved. If we relate this to the identification (fusion) of the images of 'Dew-drop' and 'Gem', in which characteristics of transience and permanence are both asserted, we can conclude that not only is the poem vulnerable to deconstruction but that it begins to deconstruct itself. Deconstructive critics consider that such marks of 'indeterminacy' in a text tend to confirm their theory.

The contrast between the two approaches is stark. The first treats the text as the focus of a uniquely articulated consciousness, which achieves realisation by taking over the reader's consciousness. The second empties the text of all identity or essential qualities, and searches for the inevitable marks of the text's failure to preserve the rules it has set up for itself. Both are reader-oriented in some sense: Poulet's reader is the text's host, while Derrida's follows and facilitates the text's self-undoing.

Section 15

Text: Wallace Stevens, 'A High-toned Old Christian Woman'
Theories: Norman Holland (ego psychology) and Roland Barthes (the plural text)

Certain key Romantic concepts found new expression in the New Criticism of Cleanth Brooks, Allen Tate, W. K. Wimsatt, John Crowe Ransom and others. A central term of this tradition was *unity*. The New Critics believed that the literary critic's task is to discover the principle of unity which integrates the disparate elements of a text. In a good poem every detail makes a contribution to the whole. Even when the details of a poem are grouped in multifarious and contradictory patterns, the critic should search for the theme which brings conflicting elements into unity. This approach assumes that the meaning inheres *in the poem* and that the critic can point to objective evidence in the poem to prove it. Since the 1960s several types of 'reader-response' criticism have developed in Europe and America. They all challenge the assumptions of New Criticism about the text's autonomy. According to most reader-response critics the meaning of a text and even the identification of a work's major features have no objective existence because they are not independent of the reader's activity. What we see in a text is bound up with the way we see. However, American reader-response theories often preserve notions of identity and selfhood which remain within the humanist discourse of New Criticism.

Norman Holland's influential psychoanalytic criticism (see 'Unity Identity Self Text' in *Reader-Response Criticism*, 1980) is extremely different from Lacanian versions of Freudian criticism (see section 11). His emphasis on the concepts of unity and individual identity harmonises with American traditions of thought. He agrees with the New Critics in believing that readers perceive unity in texts, but he also believes that the unity they discover is a reflection of their personal 'identity themes'. He suggests (following the psychological theories of Erik Erikson and Heinz Lichtenstein) that mothers imprint 'primary identities' upon their offspring and that as they mature their children build a final 'identity theme' which remains an underlying structure. The adult cannot depart from the theme but can effect certain modulations (like variations on a theme). An identity theme is like the principle of unity in a literary work. Holland argues that the unity we discover in a text is related to our identity themes. In other words, 'interpretation is a function of identity'. He goes on to describe this process of interpretation in terms of three levels:

1. Shaping the work to fit the pattern of our own defensive and adaptive strategies.
2. Discovering in the work fantasies which gratify us.
3. Transforming the work from the level of crude gratification to the level of aesthetic or philosophical unity.

His third and final level resembles the approach of the New Critics, but Holland regards it as a rationalisation of the deeper process described in levels 1 and 2.

Rather than elaborate this abstract summary I will attempt to suggest how it applies to readings of Wallace Stevens' 'A High-toned Old Christian Woman'. Here is the poem:

> Poetry is the supreme fiction, madame.
> Take the moral law and make a nave of it
> And from the nave build haunted heaven. Thus,
> The conscience is converted into palms,
> Like windy citherns hankering for hymns.
> We agree in principle. That's clear. But take
> The opposing law and make a peristyle,
> And from the peristyle project a masque
> Beyond the planets. Thus, our bawdiness,
> Unpurged by epitaph, indulged at last,
> Is equally converted into palms,
> Squiggling like saxophones. And palm for palm,
> Madame, we are where we began. Allow
> Therefore, that in the planetary scene
> Your disaffected flagellants, well-stuffed,
> Smacking their muzzy bellies in parade,
> Proud of such novelties of the sublime,
> Such tink and tank and tunk-a-tunk-tunk,
> May, merely may, madame, whip from themselves
> A jovial hullabaloo among the spheres.
> This will make widows wince: But fictive things
> Wink as they will. Wink most when widows wince.
> (From *The Collected Poems of Wallace Stevens* (Faber and Faber, London, 1923))

Most readers would no doubt notice that Stevens sets up a comparison between religion and poetry which develops in an unexpected way. The 'moral law' is compared with the 'opposing law' (the aesthetic or hedonistic). By calling poetry 'the supreme fiction' Stevens (for simplicity we shall treat the speaker in the poem as the poet) immediately challenges the old Christian woman he is addressing. A Christian normally reserves the term 'supreme' to describe God. Christianity is built upon the moral law and its structure (represented by the 'nave' of a church) points to heaven, while the opposing law, which is pagan and sensuous, is expressed in a 'peristyle' (an open and sociable architectural form associated with pagan temples) and in worldly revels ('masques') rather than 'hymns'. The 'palms' of the Christian tradition are associated with a heavenly paradise, and are matched by the pagan (earthly) 'palms,/Squiggling like saxophones'.

If we adopt Holland's theory and consider for a moment how readers might begin to interpret this poem, we may begin to see that different strategies for interpreting poems can be related to different psychological dispositions ('identity themes'). I shall invent two rather contrasted types of reader for the sake of expository vividness. One reader might see the poem as representing a challenge to Puritan moral conventions from the viewpoint of art and worldly experience, while another might see it as suggesting that the poetic imagination, in its freedom from moral convention, builds a *parallel* world to the religious world and even shares a common essence with it. From the viewpoint of the first reader, Stevens' remark 'We agree in principle' is entirely specious or ironic, while for the second it has a wry sort of truth about it. The question then arises – how can we explain the differences between these two interpretations of the poem's basic meaning? To follow the method recommended by Holland we would need to examine actual cases, which would involve looking at sample interpretations and comparing them with the identity themes of the readers (see his *5 Readers Reading*, 1975). The foundation of the approach would be a clinical study of the individuals' life histories, a study resulting in the definition of identity themes. Here we can only give hypothetical examples. Taking up Holland's theory, we might say that the more subversive reader of Stevens' poem may have an identity theme which requires the maintenance of a hostile distance between the forces of conscience (or law) and the drives and needs which go against conscience and law. This type of identity theme may reflect a deep sense of guilt about instinctual feelings and a fear of allowing these feelings to be inspected by moral conscience. Such a reader will need to *adapt* the poem to this theme by keeping the 'moral law' and 'opposing law' at a distance, allowing only a relationship of hostility or alienation to exist between them. In contrast, the reader who sees in the poem a cancelling of the differences between religious and poetic imagination may possess an identity theme which copes with guilt and anxiety by refusing to recognise the existence of authority and by regarding all claims of moral purity as fundamentally dishonest or self-deluding. An identity theme which works in this way will tend to adapt the poem to patterns of resolution and synthesis rather than of conflict and division. The essential point is that both readers will discover a pattern of meanings which corresponds to their respective identity themes. They will then be able to discover forms of gratification which their drives seek out (level 2), and finally to rise to a satisfying integration of the poem in terms of aesthetic or intellectual patterns (level 3). The first reader, for example, will be able to enjoy fantasies of flouting authority (level 2). However, on the third level, such a reader might arise above the crude satisfactions of fantasy to discover an intellectually harmonious pattern of contrasts, antitheses or ironies which knit the poem together into a pleasing unity.

Holland's theory offers an explanation of the variety of interpretations which the same text can produce, and overcomes the New Critical insistence on intrinsic textual meaning. However, he simply reintroduces the troublesome concept of unity on another level. His approach assumes that all readers look for and discover the unity in texts by appropriating them to their personal identity themes. Unity becomes a projection of an identity theme. Poststructuralists deny this assumption in fundamental ways. They argue that reading for unity always involves mastery, closure and an arbitrary limitation of meaning. They deny that the human psyche possesses the sort of unity which ego-psychology attributes to it. Lacan, for example, regards the 'subject' as a divided structure: 'I' stand at the axis of the signifier and the signified, a split being, totally unable to grasp a full 'presence'. This means that the idea of a unifying 'identity theme' is a mirage: we can discover it only through massive repression of the disruptive unconscious processes.

Roland Barthes' poststructuralist phase was devoted to exploring the unstable and unpredictable aspects of writing. His approach resembles Lacan's, but is addressed to *textual* processes, not psychological ones; he is interested in the text's 'unconscious', so to speak. Barthes would probably have considered Stevens' poem as an avant-garde text which typically encourages the reader to produce meanings by following the defiles of the signifier (see section 10). The ideal avant-garde text 'is a galaxy of signifiers, not a structure of signifieds; it has no beginning; . . . we gain access by several entrances, none of which can be authoritatively declared to be the main one' (Barthes, *S/Z*, 1975, p. 5). Stevens' poem leans towards this ideal.

In what sense does the signifier predominate in the poem? In what Barthes calls the 'readerly' (or realistic) text the signifiers are forced into apparent submission: every signifier has its appropriate and single signified. The world of such texts seems to require nothing of the reader except compliance. Stevens' poem, in contrast, is a 'writerly' text: it invites the reader to be productive and to respond to the signifiers' seductive openness. The reader can 'enjoy' the poem. What Barthes calls the 'pleasure of the text' consists in this freedom of the reader to produce meanings, and in a sense to 'write' the text. Take the signifier 'palms', for example. The repeated phrase 'converted into palms' appears to assign 'palms' a single signified, but in fact when Stevens writes that 'our bawdiness' is 'equally converted into palms' he is using the word 'equally' in a witty and perverse sense. There is no equivalence between the palms of religion and the palms of bawdiness. The second palms are 'Squiggling like saxophones'. Here we have an image of the free expression of desire (squiggles are undisciplined curvy lines). The image actually reinforces the idea of the signifier's freedom. The reader is compelled to 'produce' meaning from the play of signifiers. A more controlled play of meaning is evident in the puns 'converted' and 'project'.

The last part of the poem introduces the image of 'disaffected flagellants'. Psychologists have often commented upon the strange pleasures which some violently ascetic believers have found in self-laceration. The poet wittily presents the flagellants as hypocritically religious, proud of their 'sublime' deeds (compare 'supreme') which are actually self-indulgent and which turn out to be potentially laughable. The signifiers in this part of the poem are exceedingly 'open' – they invite several (sometimes contradictory) interpretations. Consider 'disaffected', 'stuffed', 'smacking', 'muzzy bellies', 'parade', 'tink and tank and tunk-a-tunk-tunk'. 'Disaffected' from what? We usually think of flagellants as thin ascetic types. Why therefore 'stuffed'? Is 'smacking' a playful or a serious action? Are the 'bellies' 'muzzy' from too much wine, or from moral confusion? The last signifiers ('tink and tank', etc.)

have no conventional signifieds. They may onomatopoeicly refer to the smacking of bellies (flagellation), but they are so far removed from the sound of flagellation as to suggest a more general signification – the free expression of the disaffected, the random play of the imagination. The flagellants' apparently 'sublime' rituals are so lacking in firm meanings and closed significances that they may well create 'A jovial hullabaloo among the spheres' (not at all the pious music of hymns).

The final couplet is no less 'writerly'. The play of signifiers is immediately apparent in the phonetically similar 'wink' and 'wince' (also 'will'). The common-sense connotations of the words are totally at odds: 'wink' goes with 'bawdiness', 'masques' and 'bellies', suggesting sly and jolly indulgence, while 'wince' suggests a pained moral reaction to such behaviour. 'Wince' and 'wink' are virtually the same signifier. Earlier, one signifier ('palm') is assigned two different sets of signifieds but still allowed its similarity ('palm for palm'). At another level the similarity between signifiers (wince/wink) enforces a poetic similarity of signifieds; both religion and poetry produce a superstructure of be-haviour and a range of physical expressions. Their structures are the same ('We agree in principle', 'palm for palm,/Madame, we are where we began'). The poem's indulgent playfulness at the level of the signifier is in this sense part of its meaning: opposites are both the same *and* different.

The two approaches to the poem we have considered are clearly in conflict. The first assumes that both readers and poems possess 'unity', even though the unity of poems is a by-product of the identities of readers. Barthes also treats readers as the producers of poems but for him neither text nor reader possesses identity or unity: the 'writerly' text is true to the nature of all signifying processes in refusing to limit the possibilities of meaning which the signifiers allow. Holland's approach encourages a search for the psychological identity themes which direct readers to discover unities in texts. Barthes' theory explains why texts can never possess unity. Both critics reject the 'objectivity' of the text: they argue that the reader produces a meaning or significance which is not 'in' the text.

Section 16

Text: Edgar Allan Poe, *The Fall of the House of Usher*

Theories: Jonathan Culler (the structuralist reader) and Roland Barthes (the codes)

The New Critics treated literary texts as organic forms which could be objectively analysed. They excluded from consideration the subjective act of reading (I. A. Richards and William Empson were exceptions). There has always been a common-sense reaction to this 'objectivist' attitude: surely we cannot dismiss individual reactions to a text? Can we exclude the reader's own associations, or state of mind at the time of reading? Such objections are naturally irritating especially to professional critics who don't regard the purely personal or private dimension of reading as a legitimate object of study. Psychological types of reader-response theory sometimes take account of the purely personal reactions that readers make when reading. David Bleich, for example, believes that all our so-called objective statements about literature are founded upon a *subjective* response, which motivates any subsequent critical judgements we may formulate. The structuralist tradition in literary theory treats the responses of readers not as merely personal but as essentially rule-governed. When we read, we silently (and perhaps unconsciously) follow certain shared procedures.

Jonathan Culler's *Structuralist Poetics* (1975) and *The Pursuit of Signs* (1981) explore 'poetics' rather than 'interpretation'. He does not believe that the task of structuralists is to provide yet more interpretations or to adjudicate existing interpretations. We cannot, he argues, discover *the* structure of a particular text, because it is evident that different readers discover different structures in what they read. What can be observed is the fact that readers display a 'literary competence' (which resembles linguistic competence) in their interpretive activity: they seem to know what to do when faced with a literary text. Culler's first book gave the impression that literary competence was a unified and universal phenomenon (see *Structuralist Poetics*, chapter 6). The second book accepts that there are different 'interpretive communities': different sets of rules and operations produce different sorts of interpretation (see *The Pursuit of Signs*, p. 51). Culler believes that structuralist poetics should explain the different responses readers make to the same texts. He postulates that different interpretations are to be explained by the existence of different rules and conventions of interpretation. He avoids consideration of the historical factors which determine reading conventions, since this might threaten the entire structuralist endeavour. The analogy between the linguistic system and the structure of interpretation can hold only if the structure is conceived ahistorically as a set of operational rules. For this reason, structuralists have to treat the reader as an ideal construct and not as a historically conditioned individual. I shall ignore these problems in the following application of Culler's theory.

Our passage for discussion is the opening paragraph of Edgar Allan Poe's 'The Fall of the House of Usher' (1840):

> During the whole of a dull, dark, and soundless day in the autumn of the year, when the clouds hung oppressively low in the heavens, I had been passing alone, on horseback, through a singularly dreary tract of country, and at length found myself, as the shades of the evening drew on, within view of the melancholy House of Usher. I know not how it was – but, with the first glimpse of the building, a sense of insufferable gloom pervaded my spirit. I say insufferable; for the feeling was unrelieved by any of that half-pleasurable, because poetic, sentiment with which the mind usually receives even the sternest natural images of the desolate or terrible. I looked upon the scene before me – upon the mere house, and the simple landscape features of the domain – upon the bleak walls – upon the vacant eye-like windows – upon a few rank sedges – and upon a few white trunks of decayed trees – with an utter depression of soul which I can compare to no earthly sensation more properly than to the after-dream of the reveller upon opium – the bitter lapse into every-day life – the hideous dropping off of the veil. There was an iciness, a sinking, a sickening of the heart – an unredeemed dreariness of thought which no goading of the imagination could torture into aught of the sublime. What was it – I paused to think – what was it that so unnerved me in the contemplation of the House of Usher? It was a mystery all insoluble; nor could I grapple with the shadowy fancies that crowded upon me as I pondered. I was forced to fall back upon the unsatisfactory conclusion, that while, beyond doubt, there *are* combinations of very simple natural objects which have the power of thus affecting us, still the analysis of this power lies among considerations beyond our depth. It was possible, I reflected, that a mere different arrangement of the particulars of the scene, of the details of the picture, would be sufficient to modify, or perhaps to annihilate its capacity for sorrowful impression; and, acting upon this idea, I reined my horse to the precipitous brink of a black and lurid tarn that lay in unruffled lustre by the dwelling, and gazed down – but with a shudder even more thrilling than

before – upon the remodelled and inverted images of the gray sedge, and the ghastly tree-stems, and the vacant and eye-like windows.
(From *The Complete Stories and Poems* (Doubleday, Garden City, New York, 1966, pp. 177–8))

It is clear that in order to read this at all readers must make certain fundamental and largely unconscious assumptions. The phrase 'in the autumn of the year' immediately requires us to make an adjustment to the conventions of narrative time. 'The year' is not specified; it is the year in question – the year of the time of which the narrator is speaking – a non-specific fictional time. The phrase says no more than 'in the autumn', but, if 'of the year' had been omitted, the abruptness of the conventional non-specific time would have been more striking, and therefore less easily processed. We would have asked 'which autumn?' As it is, we pass over 'in the autumn of the year' without trouble, even though we are given no specific year. Modern readers must adjust directly to 'on horseback' by assuming either that they are reading a historical novel (set in the past), or that the writer was writing before the automobile. It is unlikely that readers would assume that the rider is modern and is travelling such a distance merely for the sport or exercise, or because his car has broken down. This type of reader adjustment is not worth discussing further, even though it needs to be pointed out; a great deal of processing activity is involved in all reading and especially in the reading of fiction.

A common assumption which directs reading is that literary texts always aim at *unity* (for criticisms of this view see section 15). We often read in the expectation that the various elements in the text will form some kind of unity and are not merely decorative or random. However, there are many ways in which unity may be produced by the reader from the textual material. A reader-oriented structuralist assumes that the unity is not something present in the text but is a strategy or convention which readers may use when trying to interpret a text. We might, for example, argue that Poe's opening description establishes a *thematic* unity which runs through the entire story: everything contributes to the theme of a mysterious and sinister unity of the universe. This theme is embodied already in the very title – *The Fall of the House of Usher*. According to the local peasantry the 'House of Usher' included 'both the family and the family mansion'. The opening uses a familiar literary convention – the 'pathetic fallacy' – which assumes that natural events reflect human events. Gloomy epithets are relentlessly piled up: 'dull, dark', 'oppressively low', 'singularly dreary' and so on. The building and its surrounding landscape partake of the same atmosphere: 'bleak walls', 'black and lurid tarn', 'ghastly tree-stems'. The building itself has human features – 'vacant eye-like windows'. The gloom is most intensely focused upon the narrator's own consciousness. He is unable to grasp the reason why the scene makes such a sickening impression. What is apparent is the mysterious *unity* which links sky, landscape, House and humanity. Everything culminates in the story's final sentence in which the House is swallowed up in the tarn after its collapse following the death of Usher himself. The family, the landscape and the house become one in a 'Fall' which combines natural (autumnal) and physical connotations of collapse.

When faced with obstacles to reading caused by surprising or unexpected elements in the text, readers need to employ different strategies. Two obvious obstacles present themselves in the Poe paragraph. First, the narrator compares his 'depression of soul' to 'the after-dream of the reveller upon opium – the bitter lapse into every-day life – the hideous dropping off of the veil'. We first expect 'after-dream' to represent the nightmare of an addict. However, this 'dream' turns out to be the addict's waking to 'every-day life'. A strategy for dealing with comparisons is to look for a significant parallel between elements in the comparison. This might produce more than one result:

1. opium dream	vs	after-dream
normality	vs	depression of soul
2. revelling in opium dream	vs	bitter lapse into everyday life
normality	vs	depression of soul

We need to use a further strategy which will help us to choose the parallel most likely to produce a 'natural' meaning (on 'naturalisation' see section 6). If we pick up the antithesis between 'revelling' and 'bitter', this enables us to see the analogy in terms of a shift from happiness (revelry) to gloom (bitter lapse). In other words, we find a strategy which removes awkwardness; we can suppress the difficult parallel between opium addiction and normality.

The other obstacle is the passage in which the narrator describes his attempt to rearrange the particulars of the scene by viewing them in the tarn. Far from removing the horror, the reflected image produces an 'even more thrilling' shudder. There is no explanation of this unexpected effect. Why should a reflected image be more frightening than the image itself? A strategy for coping with this narrative puzzle is to assume that there will emerge a significance in the 'black and lurid tarn' which is not yet apparent. In other words, we assume that what is not explained *will* be explained. This strategy is finally vindicated by the story's last sentence: 'and the deep and dank tarn at my feet closed sullenly and silently over the fragments of the House of Usher.' 'Deep and dank tarn' echoes 'black and lurid tarn' fulfilling the reader's expectations. Of course, the strategy might have failed; in which case a different strategy would have been called for.

The French structuralist Roland Barthes developed a theory of 'codes' in his celebrated *S/Z* (1975). The codes represent systems of meaning which the reader activates in response to the text. The systems are not unified or totalised: they are the 'wake' or afterwash of the 'already written'. Our use of the codes does not result in the revelation of a *structure* in the text, but rather in a 'structuration' – an activation of the text's signifiers. Although this reading process is in response to the text, it cannot result in an interpretation or a fixing of meaning, because the text is only a portion of the 'already written' awaiting the reader's uniting of text to the 'general text'. There are five codes: hermeneutic, semic, symbolic, proairetic and cultural. We will illustrate Barthes' method by applying three of them to Poe's text. The hermeneutic code is concerned with 'enigma', the problem or puzzle or unanswered question which is set in motion whenever a narrator gets under way. This code is directly thematised in Poe's story: 'It was a mystery all insoluble'. All mystery and detective stories ('Whodunits') work by thematising this code. The enigma in Poe's story poses several questions: why is the scene frightening? Why is the tarn's reflection more terrifying than what it reflects? Later the question turns towards Usher's own fate: what does *he* fear and what will happen to him? The code works by *delaying* the solution to the enigma by giving false clues, by giving partial answers, by equivocating, or by jamming. When the narrator declares 'I know not how it was but . . .', 'It was a mystery all insoluble' and 'analysis . . . beyond our depth', he is *jamming* the solution to the enigma. The mysterious episode of the terrifying reflection in the tarn is an *equivocating* use of the hermeneutic code. An answer to the mystery is half hinted: the tarn is the ultimate destination of the doomed house. We are not told this directly, but it half anticipates the novel's denouement.

The symbolic code concerns the binary oppositions (see section 7) associated with certain fundamentals of existence – the human body, gender, economic divisions and so on. In Balzac's story *Sarrasine*, discussed in *S/Z*, La Zambinella is a castrato, whose ambiguous sexual identity is the centre of a great deal of symbolic play. The symbolic code often highlights the *transgression* of 'natural' boundaries. In Poe's story the boundary between human and non-human is transgressed. This is marked in the 'eye-like windows' of the house which point towards the merging of human and non-human. The house has a fissure running down it from roof to ground, which opens up like a wound when Usher falls to the ground. Usher refers to the demoralising effect of the building's 'physique'. This personification of the house relates to his belief in the 'sentience of all vegetable things'. He thinks that the unique and ghastly 'atmosphere' around the house shares this 'sentience'. The story concerns the complete overriding of the boundary between the categories of 'human' and 'inanimate'.

The cultural code is concerned with *references* to intellectual commonplaces, stereotypes, proverbs, sayings and all assumed social wisdom. Poe's narrator calls upon this code when he says 'the feeling was unrelieved by any of that half-pleasurable, because poetic, sentiment'. The reference is to the literary and aesthetic concept of the 'sublime' (mentioned explicitly a few sentences later). It is registered as 'cultural' by the locution '*that* half-pleasurable . . . sentiment'. The word 'that' marks a *reference* which the reader is assumed to be able to recognise.

Barthes' approach is 'poststructuralist' in the sense that he does not believe that any definite structure of meaning can be established either in the text or in the reader. Culler's notion of reader strategies is half-way towards a 'poststructuralist' view, since he too rejects the idea of textual structures. For Culler, reading works because readers know how to read: they possess literary competence. His approach could be radicalised by asking questions about the institutional and ideological foundations of literary competence (he has turned to these questions recently). For Barthes, reading is a sort of writing, which involves 'producing' the texts' signifiers by allowing them to be caught up in the network of codes. Barthes' theory of codes has been adapted to various radical types of criticism which seem to disrupt traditional concepts of literature and of unified meaning.

Section 17

Text: Harold Pinter, *The Homecoming*
Theory: Wolfgang Iser (Reception Theory)

The New Critics (see section 2) believed in the autonomy of the literary text. In the famous essays on the 'Intentional Fallacy' and the 'Affective Fallacy', Wimsatt and Beardsley developed powerful arguments against focusing attention on the text's inception in the author's intention and in the text's outcome in the reader's response. They accepted that readers do experience emotional responses to what they read, but they added that the emotional impact of a literary work is always determined by objective features in the text. If we experience despair, exaltation, hilarity, or calmness, these responses can be traced to stylistic or other technical aspects of the work. Our response, they argued, has its foundation in an achieved aesthetic structure of emotion in the work. They concluded that the job of the critic was to examine this intrinsic and objective 'emotion' and not the subjective experience of the reader which may, in any case, be quite inappropriate or misguided.

During the 1960s a reaction to these views developed. A wide range of reader-response theories evolved which were based on different theoretical foundations but which all shared a conviction that a text's meaning and significance was intimately bound up with the activity of the reader. They argued that a literary text is not like a monument or objective entity with a fixed set of characteristics which the reader simply takes in at a glance. Texts are full of gaps, blanks, ambiguities, indeterminacies, which the reader must fill, close up, or develop. Some reader-response critics place an emphasis on the reader's contribution to a text's meaning, while others recognise that there are 'triggers' in the text which direct the reader's interpretive activity. Wolfgang Iser solves the problem by distinguishing between the 'implied reader', whom the text creates for itself through 'response-inviting structures' which predispose us to read in certain ways, and the 'actual reader' who brings to the act of reading a certain stock of experiences which colour the reading process.

Harold Pinter's *The Homecoming* opens with a scene between Max, a seventy-year-old widower and father of three sons, and Lenny his thirty-year-old second son. Having failed to gain Lenny's attention over a missing pair of scissors, Max continues in rambling fashion:

> I think I'll have a fag. Give me a fag.
> *Pause.*
> Look what I'm lumbered with.
> *He takes out a crumpled cigarette from his pocket.*
> I'm getting old, my word of honour.
> *He lights it.*
> You think I wasn't a tearaway? I could have taken care of you, twice over. I'm still strong. You ask your Uncle Sam what I was. But at the same time I always had a kind heart. Always.
> *Pause.*
> I used to knock about with a man called MacGregor. I called him Mac. You remember Mac? Eh?
> *Pause.*
> Huhh! We were two of the worst hated men in the West End of London. I tell you, I still got the scars. We'd walk into a place, the whole room'd stand up, they'd make way to let us pass. You never heard such silence. Mind you, he was a big man, he was over six foot tall. His family were all MacGregors, they came all the way from Aberdeen, but he was the only one they called Mac.
> *Pause.*
> He was very fond of your mother, Mac was. Very fond. He always had a good word for her.
> *Pause.*
> Mind you, she wasn't such a bad woman. Even though it made me sick just to look at her rotten stinking face, she wasn't such a bad bitch. I gave her the best bleeding years of my life anyway.
> Lenny. Plug it, will you, you stupid sod, I'm trying to read the paper.
> Max. Listen! I'll chop your spine off, you talk to me like that! You understand? Talking to your lousy filthy father like that!
> Lenny. You know what, you're getting demented.
> *Pause.*
> What do you think of Second Wind for the three-thirty?
> Max. Where?
> Lenny. Sandown Park.
>
> (From *The Homecoming* (Methuen, London, 1965, pp. 8–9))

I will not employ a particular reader-response theory at first, but simply point out the usefulness of such approaches. In discussing drama the reader must, of course, become the audience. First consider the pauses. A formalist – a New Critic or Russian Formalist, for example – would treat the pauses as structural elements in the dramatic text whose effects should be capable of being objectively assessed. From this point of view we might say that Pinter (or rather the text) *implies* that certain unspoken thoughts or feelings exist as sub-texts. Audiences would therefore be expected to try to grasp these meanings when they interpret the pauses. From the viewpoint of reader-oriented criticism this attitude is absurd. The pauses are clearly *indeterminate*: there is no objective meaning which can be grasped when we contemplate them. It is in the very nature of such moments of silence that the audience must actively fill them with significance or meaning.

To take an example, one of the pauses separates two of Max's remarks about his dead wife Jessie: (1) Mac 'always had a good word for her'; (2) 'Mind you, she wasn't such a bad woman'. The first statement, considering Mac and Max were supposed to be buddies, seems entirely positive, implying that Jessie was a good woman. The second statement appears to imply the need to defend Jessie from criticism. Only the audience can fill the blank between the two statements. For example, we may interpolate as Max's thought during the pause – 'I can't imagine why Mac was so fond of her'. This would account for the apparent switch to a tone of justification. A second possibility would arise if we treat Max's 'Mind you' as an idiosyncratic piece of grammar. Rather than being contrastive in significance the phrase could mean simply 'And what is more'. The previous use of the phrase ('Mind you, he was a big man') doesn't appear to have a contrastive force either. This means that we would interpret the pause as conveying the thought 'This fondness of Mac's was perfectly understandable'. Clearly there are other ways in which an audience could fill this gap.

It begins to look as though readers and audiences can fill in blanks just about in any way they choose. Is this really so? Well, clearly not. Both my suggested 'actualisations' are very precisely relatable to the text's 'response-inviting structures'. Not only that but when we first read or watch the play we are dependent on the *unfolding vistas* of the scenes as they succeed one another, in order to shape our interpretations of characters (and even of pauses). The pause we have been discussing would be seen retrospectively in a different perspective when, at the end of the play, we hear of Jessie's adultery with Mac. If we assume that Max knew of this, it would explain his obvious ambivalence towards his dead wife. The first way of filling the pause ('I can't imagine why Mac was so fond of her') would be transformed to something like 'I'm not surprised that the bastard always had a good word for my bitch of a wife'. This interpretation also fits the odd disgust expressed in Max's ensuing words. What is clear from our discussion so far is that the pauses can be filled in various ways (though not in any way we choose) and that the changing perspectives of the play will alter our interpretation retrospectively.

I have just been using an approach proposed by the German theorist Wolfgang Iser, who argues, in *The Act of Reading* (1978), that 'the reader's communication with the text is a dynamic process of self-correction, as he formulates signifieds which he must then continually modify.' We grasp what we read only as a series of changing viewpoints. At any given stage in reading there are always a number of possible ways of building a provisional interpretation of the characters and their situation. We may at one stage form a sense of the situation which may need to be reassessed later. The reader is always looking forwards and backwards at the same time. Our construction of meaning is likely to be open and provisional at the outset, but to become gradually less open and more definite. To return to our example of Max's thoughts about Jessie, as we proceed through the play we reduce the number of perspectives and possibilities of meaning which attach to Max's words and his silences. However, it is one of Pinter's skills to frustrate this process of deduction.

Iser's studies are mainly devoted to the novel, in which 'consistency building' by the reader is perhaps easier to achieve. In drama there is no narrator, and no way in which characters can be delineated except by implication. Pinter's play retains the maximum of indeterminacy at every point, leaving the audience free to fill the many 'gaps' of indeterminacy, relatively unassisted by textual triggers. Consider the earlier part of Max's soliloquy (from 'I'm getting older' to 'I still got the scars'). The audience has just met Max and has very little to go on in building a 'gestalt' (image of the whole) of Max as a character. In this passage we have:

1. His acknowledgement of waning powers in old age.
2. His denial of waning powers ('I'm still strong').
3. His claim to kind-heartedness.
4. His pride in his past reputation (along with Mac) of being tough.

As we pass through the sequence of utterances we are forced to continually modify our image of Max. The speech does not provide connecting links between the various statements. Only the audience can supply these links. As Iser shows, we fill these gaps according to our existing 'stock of experience' and our 'world-view'. At the same time we adjust our perspective on Max as the play unfolds and gives us different viewpoints.

The process of reading involves both a *response* to the text's structure (the work is unfolded in a certain manner) and an active *'actualisation'* of the 'gaps of indeterminacy' in the text. We are guided by the text and at the same time we bring the text into realisation as meaning at every point. Iser's 'reception theory' is an attempt to integrate textual analysis with 'affective' criticism. Its strength lies in its dynamic approach to the process of reading: the text ceases to be treated as a static object and becomes a changing 'gestalt'. A text, no longer a timeless aesthetic object, is experienced as an unfolding temporal sequence. Even though Iser tends to play down the ideological questions which arise when we examine the different ways in which readers fill gaps, his account of reading at the micro-level is unsurpassed.

Section 18

Texts: Arnold Wesker, *Roots*, and Samuel Beckett, *Endgame*
Theory: Hans Robert Jauss (Reception Theory)

In several chapters I have treated the New Critical approach to the study of literary texts as a typical stalking-horse of more recent theories. Sometimes a positive sense of difference was consciously entertained by modern critics when they formulated their approaches. This is especially true of reader-response critics, who rebelled against the New Critics' belief that the proper object of critical study was the work's intrinsic literary properties. In 'The Affective Fallacy' Wimsatt and Beardsley dismissed the reader's response as at worst a mere 'personal registration' and at best a response constructed from the text's formal properties. In Section 17 we saw that Iser did not altogether reject the New Critics' ideas when he allowed for those 'response-inviting structures' which direct the reading process, but he also tried to theorise the reader's positive contribution to making sense of texts, particularly by filling the 'gaps' which occur in all discourse.

In his *Toward an Aesthetic of Reception* (1982, chapter 1), Hans Robert Jauss, the German theorist, reacts strongly against those who view the literary text as a monumental object or who see meaning as fixed once and for all. He rejects the idea that texts await an endless sequence of attempts to get at their meaning which lies within them like the kernel of a nut. Like the structuralists (especially Jonathan Culler), Jauss believes that the fact of disagreement about meaning needs to be explained. New Critics and other formalists assume that readers disagree because some of them are not attending to the literary aspect of literature. Jauss observes that the most interesting disagreements are those which exist over long periods of time. It is clear that eighteenth-century readings of Shakespeare differ from twentieth-century readings to an extent which goes beyond mere differences of personality or class. What is more, there are strong affinities between *all* eighteenth-century readings of Shakespeare. This is apparent to us from the distant perspective of the twentieth century. Jauss helpfully draws upon the terms 'paradigm' and 'horizon of expectations' to define this phenomenon of shared assumptions. According to the philosopher of science T. S. Kuhn, scientists in a given period work within a particular 'paradigm' of concepts and assumptions. Once a paradigm (e.g. Newtonian physics) has exhausted itself and scientists working with it have started coming up with too many unsolved problems, a new paradigm usually evolves. Similarly, argues Jauss, readers and writers in a given period read and write within a set of assumptions and conventions which governs their practice. The assumptions include those about literature (about the nature of genres, style, form and so on) and about the contexts of literature. The contemporary readers of a particular text read it within a dominant 'horizon of expectations' which may or may not be shared by the writer. If the horizon is shared, the writer will be immediately understood and easily interpreted by his contemporaries. However, at a later stage, readers may find the same text unreadable because they bring a different set of assumptions to bear upon it. The reverse can also occur: writers, such as William Blake, may be working outside the dominant literary paradigm of their day; their writings may have to await a later generation of readers for appreciation and understanding. There are cases of texts which contribute to the formation of a later horizon of expectations. Jauss's approach allows both the idea of a *shared* set of assumptions which governs practice and the idea of the *rejection* of a specific horizonal framework. In other words, his theory helps to explain change and revolution in literary history.

Finally, he raises the question of how someone reading in the present can hope to form a complete understanding of an earlier work. Clearly it would be possible to identify the various horizons which have influenced reading in earlier periods and even to attempt to identify one's own. But then, how would we arrive at a final assessment? Jauss's approach to this problem derives from the tradition of 'hermeneutics' and especially the work of Hans-Georg Gadamer, who, in *Truth and Method* (1975), tries to solve the problems of communicating with the past. For Gadamer the meaning of a text is not limited to the author's intentions but is continually extended by the later readings. He emphasises the historical *situatedness* of the reader: we are all historical beings who bring our time-bound identities to all we do. He also rejects the division between subject and object: we are not lofty neutral minds surveying the past from a Parnassian height of wisdom and objectivity. Any object we study can never be separated from our subjectivity. All we can expect to achieve when studying the sequence of horizons and readings of a particular text is a 'fusion' of horizons: my reading becomes a focusing and ordering instrument in a complex perspective of horizons going right back to the contemporary reader of the text. This fusion occurs unconsciously and inevitably as the reader's own horizon is absorbed into the process of interpretation.

In considering two modern examples I am limiting the historical span of such horizonal perspectives. I wish to concentrate on certain aspects of Jauss's theory, especially those which concern the effects of changed horizons and the reception of texts which challenge current assumptions. The first example will be concerned with the social context of the audience's reception of a play, the second with the literary horizon itself. Arnold Wesker's play *Roots* is part of a trilogy (1958–60) which deals with socialism in Britain as represented in the life of the Kahn family through its many vicissitudes during the period from 1936 (the Cable Street riots against fascism) to 1959 (the third successive election defeat of the Labour Party). In *Roots* Beatie, the daughter of a Norfolk tenant farmer, returns home full of the socialist ideas of her boyfriend Ronnie Kahn (Wesker). The Norfolk folk are rough, unromantic and down-to-earth. It is clear, for example, that, despite their narrow-mindedness about many things, they do not have very strict views about sex. Beatie and her sister Jenny take up the subject of babies:

> *Beatie.* You gonna hev another Jenny?
> *Jenny.* Well, course I am. What you on about? Think Jimmy don't want none of his own?
> *Beatie.* He's a good man Jenny.
> *Jenny.* Yearp.
> *Beatie.* Not many men would marry you after you had a baby.
> *Jenny* No.
> *Beatie.* You hevn't told no one hev you Jenny?
> *Jenny.* No, that I hevn't.
> *Beatie.* Well, that's it gal, don't you tell me then!
> (This and the following extract from *The Wesker Trilogy* (Penguin, Harmondsworth, 1964, pp. 96, 136))

In isolation this passage might appear to suggest that Jenny is very ashamed of having had an illegitimate child before marriage, but it becomes clear that her reaction is a mixture of characteristic Norfolk privacy and sheer indifference. Later, at the disastrous party when

Ronnie fails to turn up, the company discuss old Stan Mann who died earlier in the play. He represents a certain vitality and sexual honesty which is not so apparent in the younger generation. (At seventy-five he playfully threatens to have Beatie 'on a plate'.) They discuss Mrs Mann too:

> Frank.   They weren't even married were they?
> Jenny.   No, they never were – she started lookin' after him when he had that first stroke and she just stayed.
> Jimmy.   Lost her job 'cos of it too.
> Frank.   Well, yes, she would, wouldn't she – she was a State Registered Nurse or something weren't she? [to Beatie] Soon ever the authorities got to hear o' that they told her to pack up living' wi' him or quit her job, see?
> Jenny.   Bloody daft I reckon. What difference it make whether she married him or not.

The laxness of Jenny's attitude is plain: the Norfolk ideology goes against middle-class convention, even though it has its own kinds of narrowness.

I have chosen a passage about sexual mores because between the time of the play's original production (1959) and the productions of the 1970s there occurred a famous sexual revolution in a period popularly known as the 'permissive' age. During the 1960s there were also important changes affecting censorship (the *Lady Chatterley* trial and the abolition of theatre censorship). It is apparent that these changes involved a radical alteration of horizon. There is no space here to elaborate on the literary aspect of this alteration, but the attitude towards and assumptions about sexual behaviour as expressed in all the arts were certainly changed. How does all this affect the reception of the dialogues quoted above? A contemporary audience would have seen the Norfolk attitude as unconventional, slightly shocking and part of the low-life 'kitchen-sink' realism of the play. Wesker's 'Note to Actors and Producers' is carefully addressed to such a response: 'The picture I have drawn is a harsh one, yet my tone is not one of disgust.' Many post-1968 audiences would have quite different reactions to Jenny's and Stan's attitudes to sexual convention. No longer would they see Stan's vitality against the background of a dull routine of unconventionality. Even if they reject the 'permissiveness' of the 1960s the new horizon of expectations would alter the meaning of the Norfolk views, with the result that Wesker's intentions as expressed in the Note may be difficult to communicate in a production: the sense of 'harshness' which he points out may well fade or disappear. Looking back thirty years from the play's original production can we arrive at a final meaning? Or are we faced with the possibility that as new horizons of expectations evolve, the text's meaning (as expressed in productions) will also change? Jauss's solution is to suggest that our historically-determined perspective enters and fuses with preceding perspectives. The concept of 'fusion' is highly problematic, and seems to deny the possibility that we might acquire 'knowledge' of history. It is worth adding that Jauss warns us against a naïve reflectionist view of literature and history: literary works are capable of intervening and shaping social values at least as much as merely reflecting them. It is possible that the 'kitchen-sink' drama of the late 1950s actually prepared the ground for the 'permissive' 1960s. One of the difficulties involved in Jauss's approach is related to this very fluidity and instability of horizons. Elements both in the work and in the audience may be 'out-of-time' in the sense that they are not in accord with the prevailing horizon of expectations.

The notion of horizonal discord is especially relevant to the study of avant-garde writing. What is avant-garde when read in one period may become the norm within another. The plays of Samuel Beckett were incomprehensible to audiences when they were first seen. However, in the long run, their departures from conventional expectations contributed to horizonal change. In *Endgame* the two main characters Hamm and Clov are living out what seem to be the final stages of their existence: Hamm is the blind, chair-bound master, and Clov the lame servant who carries out the minimal wishes of Hamm. Here is a typical exchange:

Hamm. The waves, how are the waves?
Clov. The waves? (*He turns the telescope on the waves.*) Lead.
Hamm. And the sun?
Clov. (*looking*). Zero.
Hamm. But it should be sinking. Look again.
Clov. (*looking*). Damn the sun.
Hamm. Is it night already then?
Clov. (*looking*). No. [. . . .]
(*Clov returns to his place beside the chair.*)
Clov. Why this farce, day after day?
Hamm. Routine. One never knows. (*Pause.*) Last night I saw inside my breast. There was a big sore.
Clov. Pah! You saw your heart.
Hamm. No, it was living. (*Pause. Anguished.*) Clov!
Clov. Yes.
Hamm. What's happening?

Clov. Something is taking its course.
       Pause.
Hamm. Clov!
Clov. *(patiently).* What is it?
Hamm. We're not beginning to . . . to . . . mean something?
Clov. Mean something! You and I, mean something! *(Brief laugh.)* Ah
       that's a good one!
Hamm. I wonder. *(Pause.)* Imagine if a rational being came back to
       earth, wouldn't he be liable to get ideas into his head if he
       observed us long enough. *(Voice of rational being.)* Ah, good,
       now I see what it is, yes, now I understand what they're at!
       *(Clov starts, drops the telescope and begins to scratch his belly with
       both hands. Normal voice.)* And without going so far as that, we
       ourselves . . . *(with emotion)* . . . we ourselves . . . at certain
       moments . . . *(Vehemently.)* To think perhaps it won't all have
       been for nothing!
(From *Endgame, a Play in One Act* (Faber and Faber, London, 1958, pp.
                                                                    26–7))

In the 1950s Beckett's first British audiences came to the plays with
certain assumptions in their minds about the nature of drama, and
specifically about dramatic character and dramatic action. The plays of
the preceding generation were mainly 'realistic' in both characterisation and action. Beckett's plays did not conform at all to these
conventions. This play's action is static and repetitive, and the
characters are not individual 'personalities' but mere receptacles for
thought and emotion.

There is no sense of a naturalistic world 'out there'. The 'waves' and
the 'sun' which Clov inspects through his telescope are reduced to the
same state of blank nullity as everything else in their world. When the
characters refer to 'this farce', 'something . . . taking its course' and the
problem of 'meaning', they are not referring to any specific actuality but
to a general existential condition. When Clov says 'Something is
taking its course', the audience cannot locate this 'something' in any
naturalistic context established by the play. The characters do not
speak as real people or express coherent and continuous psychological
states of mind. Hamm's emotions ('Anguished', 'with emotion', 'Vehe-
mently') are abruptly shifting states which suggest no continuity of
personality. The audience cannot *identify* with the characters as people.
The focus is rather on the human predicament – the sense of
meaninglessness, the fading but persisting sense that there should be a
meaning in life, the absurdity of human existence ('this farce').

The audience cannot even adjust their emotions to this gloomy
existentialism, because the action often shifts gear into literal farce.

The passage we have been studying continues with Clov's discovery of a flea. Hamm is 'very perturbed': he fears that 'humanity might start from there all over again!' This grotesque piece of cosmic theorising is followed by music-hall action:

> Clov.   I'm back again, with the insecticide.
> Hamm. Let him have it!
> *Clov loosens the top of his trousers, pulls it forward and shakes*
> *powder into the aperture. He stoops, looks, waits, starts, frenzied*
> *shakes more powder, stoops, looks, waits.*

The audience is prevented from treating the action as either comic or tragic; it is absurd, which is of course now a cliché of theatre criticism. The horizon within which the first audiences received the play is quite different from that of a more recent audience. Of course, not all members of audiences have entered the new 'informed' horizon, but one should remember that Beckett's dramatic conventions have not only fed into the genre expectations of audiences but have also become part of a general 'postmodern' consciousness which draws into its discourse ideas of the holocaust and the nuclear age. It is worth adding that the French horizon of expectations within which Beckett wrote was quite different from the English one. The work of Jarry and Ionesco, for example, had already disrupted the naturalistic expectations of theatre audiences.

It is clear from this example that it is difficult, when talking about horizons, to keep purely literary expectations separate from larger historical developments. Beckett's drama both challenges the existing horizon and helps to produce a new one. Jauss's theory provides an account of literary change from the point of view of 'reception'. It helps to explain fundamental shifts in interpretation of the same texts over a period of time and the alterations in prevailing norms and conventions resulting from literary innovation.

Chapter 6

Marxist and Feminist Criticism

Section 19

Text: John Milton, *Paradise Lost*
Theory: Marxist and Feminist Criticism (The Politics of Class and Gender)

This chapter introduces Marxist and feminist critical approaches by examining their application to passages from John Milton's epic poem *Paradise Lost* (1667). Both Marxists and feminists adopt a 'conflict model' of society. Our individual roles and identities are not the outcome of a unified culture and an organic social process but are produced by a fundamentally unjust and oppressive social organisation. Marxists believe that human self-realisation is blocked by class domination at every level (economic, political and ideological). Feminists perceive women as in the position of a social class, exploited by patriarchy at all levels (economic, political, ideological). Some feminists include a Marxist strand in their explanation of women's oppression.

A Marxist reading of *Paradise Lost* could take many different forms. Among the possibilities are the following:

1. A study of the poem as an expression of seventeenth-century class conflict. This would start by reading the Civil Wars (1642–9) as a struggle between forward- and backward-looking sections of the ruling classes. The outcome of the wars is usually seen by Marxists as a victory for the bourgeois class (a victory which was not materially reversed by the restoration of the monarchy in 1660).

2. A study of the poem as an expression of Milton's personal situation after the restoration of the monarchy in 1660. As an international figure on the republican side he was seriously at risk at the time of the Restoration. From this viewpoint the poem becomes an allegory of political resistance.

3. A study of the poem's representation of Puritan ideology. 'Ideology' here is not so much the consciously stated ideas of a social

class or group but rather their 'world-view' or the imaginary forms in which they represented their society to themselves (on ideology see section 22).

Fundamental to any Marxist type of interpretation is the notion of 'determinants'. (A useful introduction to Marxist criticism is Terry Eagleton's *Marxism and Literary Criticism*, 1976.) Marx believed that social and economic realities were the ultimate determinants of culture and human consciousness. He explicitly contradicted the Hegelian theory of history which argued that 'consciousness determines life'. Later Marxists, following Engels' reformulations of Marx's theories, emphasised the 'relative autonomy' of ideology and culture. Without denying the ultimately determining effect of the social and economic level in the social formation, they allowed literature (along with other cultural forms) a certain 'specific effectivity', including its own formal development. The historical conditions of a poem's production includes ideological, social or economic determinants. An individual uneven structure of determinants will ultimately take its form from the overall developments within a particular historical mode of production. In the case of *Paradise Lost* the early emergence of the capitalist mode of production and the rise of middle-class political, cultural and economic power are the relevant historical conditions.

A Marxist theory, even a vulgar Marxist theory, would also ask specific kinds of question about the immediate context of composition. If we consider the poet's own famous declaration of intent – to 'justify the ways of God to men' – we can see how far the Marxist privileging of history affects our interpretation. A common-sense reading might treat the phrase as referring to some universal question in theology and to Milton's intention to give *his* answer to a standard problem facing all believers. By contextualising the author's statement of intent, we make it historically specific: why should Milton concern himself with this problem in the period immediately following the Restoration of the monarchy in England? Why should God's ways need justifying at this juncture? The historical answer is a fairly obvious one: the failure of the Commonwealth, the defeat of the free-born Reason of the Puritan leaders, and the restoration of monarchy required a theological explanation. Why did God dash the hopes of his chosen people? Simply by posing these questions a Marxist theory of literature and society directs our reading towards aspects of the poem which would otherwise appear marginal. The poem therefore becomes not a timeless epic of

Man's Fall but a heroic response to a situation which from the Puritan point of view was tragic in its implications. One should add that this type of contextualising, though typical of Marxist readings of literature, is not exclusively Marxist. Only in so far as an historical interpretation involves situating a cultural practice in a larger *socio-economic* development can it be regarded as 'Marxist'.

Milton had been a prominent supporter of the republican cause, even after he had given up (partly because of his blindness) his important post as Secretary for the Foreign Tongues during the Commonwealth. He continued to argue in print for the cause even when it was positively dangerous to do so. To quote Lois Potter, 'Probably the most courageous thing Milton ever did was to publish *A Ready and Easy Way to Establish a Free Commonwealth*, whose second edition appeared only a month before the return of the King' (*A Preface to Milton*, p. 27). Silenced as the leading proponent of the republican cause, Milton was compelled to respond in the coded form of religious epic. Since one would not expect either explicit political statements or a consistent allegory, interpretation is exceedingly problematic. However, the difficulty of producing a definite reading does not invalidate the attempt to read the poem in this way.

Milton's conception of true heroism centres upon the figures of Abdiel, Enoch and Noah. Like Milton himself in 1659, Abdiel was 'Among the faithless, faithful only he;/Among innumerable false, unmoved' (V.897–8). God praises him for his resistance to Satan:

> Servant of God, well done, well hast thou fought
> The better fight, who single hast maintained
> Against revolted multitudes the cause
> Of truth, in word mightier than they in arms;
> And for the testimony of truth hast borne
> Universal reproach . . .
>
> (VI.29ff.)

Abdiel's sole concern was 'To stand approved in sight of God, though worlds/Judged thee perverse'. This perfectly describes Milton's own position immediately before the Restoration. Milton, like Noah, was the 'one just man', and like Enoch, 'The only righteous in a world perverse'. What makes this approach to the poem attractive to Marxist critics is the ideological perspective which it affords: Puritan ideology in general is represented in the character of Abdiel. Another Marxist reading might include a study of Milton's insertion into a specific type of Puritan ideology. Christopher Hill, for example, in his *Milton and the*

English Revolution (1977), places Milton in an uneasy position between orthodox Puritanism and popular heretical culture. (On *Paradise Lost*, see Hill, chapters 28 and 29.)

A Marxist reading might also encourage a certain type of allegorical interpretation. Whenever censorship is in force allegory comes into its own both as a method of reading and as a method of writing. Milton often describes the fallen angels in terms which apply to the royalists. The most striking case is the portrait of Belial:

> Belial came last, than whom a spirit more lewd
> Fell not from heaven, or more gross to love
> Vice for itself [. . . .]
> In courts and palaces he also reigns
> And in luxurious cities, where the noise
> Of riot ascends above their loftiest towers,
> And injury and outrage; and when night
> Darkens the streets, then wander forth the sons
> Of Belial, flown with insolence and wine.
>
> (I.490–2, 497–502)

Professor Rajan points out (see Alastair Fowler's edition, I.490–3, note) that Belial would have been regarded by Puritans as very much the cavalier type – 'suave, dilettante, dissolute and lacking in courage'. In a sense Milton is speaking in an ideological code to his Puritan readership. The phrase 'courts and palaces' is explicit enough to point us in the right direction. In a period when the court was notorious for its sexual promiscuity and sex comedies were a popular court entertainment, it is scarcely surprising that Milton frequently used this type of allegorical moral rebuke.

Broadly, there are two kinds of feminist criticism: one is concerned with unearthing, rediscovering or re-evaluating women's writing, and the other with rereading literature from the point of view of women rather than of men. (A useful introduction is K. K. Ruthven's *Feminist Literary Studies*, 1984.) The second has a good deal to say about *Paradise Lost*. Milton's own patriarchal views are strongly expressed in the poem, although it is only fair to point out that his version of the Fall is closely modelled on the version in Genesis. Also, it should be said that in some respects the Puritan view of women was more enlightened than the Cavalier view. The latter favoured either cynical denigration of women or gallant adulation. Milton's divorce pamphlets place great emphasis upon the mutuality of affection in marriage. However, there remains in the spiritualised, Puritan view of women, which Milton shared, an engrained patriarchal attitude. Without examining the various types of feminist theory it is clear that 'reading as a woman' makes a 'critical difference'. Traditional scholars, however, including women, object strongly to the 'irrelevant' and unhistorical value judgements made by feminists when addressing classic texts such as Milton's. Indeed, the dismissal of Milton as a writer on the ground of his alleged misogyny raises awkward problems for literary criticism which cannot be addressed in this short book.

It would be possible to demonstrate several types of feminist reading of the poem, showing its patriarchal shaping of style, imagery and character. For example, in Book IV, when Satan first sees Paradise, its entrance is presented quite distinctly as female genitals:

> So on he fares, and to the border comes,
> Of Eden, where delicious Paradise,
> Now nearer, crowns with her enclosure green,
> As with a rural mound the champaign head
> Of a steep wilderness, whose hairy sides
> With thicket overgrown, grotesque and wild
> Access denied;
>
> (IV.131–7)

Rather than provide more examples of this sort, I would like to suggest that a feminist perspective yields interesting results when applied to the work of editors, who rarely escape the traps of patriarchal ideology. Alastair Fowler, perhaps the best modern editor of the poem, is no exception. It has been clearly established that while Milton may have had personal reasons for his views on the subordination of women, compared with many Puritans he was quite liberal and was much more idealistic about marriage than many. Nevertheless, modern readers can scarcely be unaware of Milton's patriarchal rendering of the Adam and Eve story. Fowler's copious notes sometimes fall silent where the female reader is most likely to be seeking editorial comment. For example, one would expect some commentary or at least the citation of authorities, on the following lines spoken by Adam:

> for nothing lovelier can be found
> In woman, than to study household good,
> And good works in her husband to promote.
>
> (IX.232–4)

This is, of course, perfectly orthodox in the seventeenth century (and is still believed by many!). Fowler at other times prefers, where possible, to justify Milton's patriarchal arguments. Nothing embodies the subordination of Eve more clearly than her withdrawal from two central scenes in which Adam receives knowledge and warnings from Raphael (Book VIII) and Michael (Book XI). In Book VIII Milton tells us that though intellectually able to follow such discourse Eve preferred to hear such matter from her husband's mouth, since he would intersperse 'conjugal caresses' and 'grateful digressions'. Fowler accepts the poet's own claim not to be implying Eve's intellectual inferiority, and adds a further justification: Milton 'may have felt the need to square his account with *1 Cor.* xiv 35: "And if they will learn anything, let them ask their husbands at home: for it is a shame for women to speak in the church"' (VIII.48–56n). If anything this citation deepens the sexist significance of Eve's withdrawal. In Book XI when Michael puts Eve to sleep and takes Adam to the hill, Fowler comments that the resemblance to Book VIII is superficial. The true parallel, he argues, is between Eve's sleep here and Adam's sleeping vision of Eve's creation in Book VIII: the earlier vision was of Eve's creation; this new vision will be of the future offspring of Eve. Once again, he supports Milton's own views and rejects as superficial what seem to be striking similarities between the two occasions when Eve is excluded from the angels' communications to Adam of knowledge of past and future. Finally, in IX, when Eve celebrates Adam's decision to die with her in the 'O glorious trial of exceeding love' speech, Fowler ingeniously finds evidence to support the author's downgrading of this speech by pointing out a blasphemous play on the theological term 'eminent' which implies a parallel between Adam's self-sacrifice and Christ's. My point about these editorial interventions and silences is not that they are without textual justification but that they all tend to support and not simply explain Milton's patriarchal assumptions. It seems to me that only a feminist critique is capable of bringing this clearly to light.

Theories examined in earlier sections have provided concepts and methods which can be applied directly to the text's linguistic surface. Marxist and feminist theories often work at a more general level, affecting the reader's overall strategies of reading. Central ideas such as 'mode of production', 'ideology' and 'patriarchy' shape the reader's framework of interpretation in fundamental ways by directing attention to the inequality with which both economic and sexual power have been shared in the past and in the present.

Section 20

Text: Kingsley Amis, *Lucky Jim*
Theory: Feminist Criticism (Reading as a Woman)

The New Criticism is the orthodoxy (more dominant in America than Britain) against which we have assessed several modern critical approaches. Feminist criticism in America was very conscious of its need to shake off the apparent objectivity of New Criticism with its insistence on the 'impersonality' of author and reader. Feminists wanted to object to the ways in which gender was represented in literature, but felt coerced by a male-dominated critical school which sanctified the male author as an impregnable author-ity, whose personal life and ideology were not relevant to the impersonal literary structures he created. A celebrated public meeting in New York in 1971 (broadcast on television under the title 'Town Bloody Hall') involved a confrontation between the novelist Norman Mailer and a group of representatives of the women's movement (including Germaine Greer). Mailer was frequently attacked as the embodiment of male fantasies and patriarchal authority. The writings of Mary Ellmann (*Thinking about Women*, 1968) and Kate Millett (*Sexual Politics*, 1969) provided plenty of ammunition against Mailer. Millett had called Mailer 'a prisoner of the virility cult'. When the discussion turned specifically to his novels, Mailer strongly objected to the way the views of his male characters were being taken to represent his own views. He cuttingly pointed out that one of the first principles of literary criticism requires the critic to separate the author from the voices of the literary work. If one of his characters uses violent phallic imagery this does not mean that Mailer himself is indulging in violent male fantasies, he argued. Indeed, he suggested, it might very well be that the intention of the author is to expose such fantasies. However, one should say in reply that, if readers find themselves attributing such fantasies to the author we must be careful not to dismiss their sense of the text's meaning. Also, there is little doubt that Mailer's novels are often significantly obsessed by male degradation of women (notably in *An American Dream*). Mailer's 'That's how it is' or 'There's no point in ignoring the power of sexuality' is, from a feminist viewpoint, an evasion of the issue.

If feminist critics are right in thinking that the history of literature has been dominated by a patriarchal authority which has demeaned women in various ways, then men cannot wriggle out of the accusation simply by claiming that their representations of women and men are completely impersonal creations reflecting the full range and diversity of human types. This defence ignores the role of the reader (often a woman addressed by a male author) in determining the significance of the author's representations. It also ignores a number of dimensions of literary texts which go beyond the mere representation of sexist attitudes. First, characterisation will inevitably involve the use (even the most sophisticated use) of stereotypes of both men and women. Secondly, the point of view (or implied author) governing the narrative in a novel will inevitably represent an overall ideology or world-view which could be patriarchal. Thirdly, it is relatively unusual, though more common in recent years, for the central characters in novels written by men to be women. The effects of seeing women always through the eyes of male heroes (or anti-heroes) are hard to recognise, especially if you are a male reader.

If we think positively in terms of reading as a woman, we immediately see that for a long time reading has assumed a male perspective and that there is a real difference of view when the experiences and values of women become central in the act of reading. (A useful introduction is Jonathan Culler's 'Reading as a woman', in *On Deconstruction*, 1983, pp. 43–64.) Of course, it is clear that women can also, and once usually did, read 'as men' – and can adopt the dominant (that is, male) reader position. This is made possible, despite the difference of female experience, because texts are produced in such a way that they *construct the reader's experience* from a certain (male) angle. For example, they produce narratives which are archetypically male (heroic adventures ending in male submission to marriage) and which situate the reader in the imaginative position of the male. Therefore, in order to read as a woman the reader has consciously to resist this construction. Being female and therefore having female life experience does not mean that one reads as a woman. In order to bring into play female experience at all, women have to actively question the way in which texts construct them as readers.

My example is a passage from Kingsley Amis's novel *Lucky Jim*. Although Jim is clearly a figure of fun, whose career is a chapter of accidents and disasters, he is nevertheless the focal male hero. Events and other characters are consistently seen from his jaundiced viewpoint. The reader is invited to be amused by and also to identify with Jim's picaresque adventures. He becomes entangled in an unwanted relationship with the dowdy Margaret who had tried to commit suicide after being ditched by Catchpole. When Jim unexpectedly starts a relationship with the glamorous Christine he decides to drop Margaret. Her reaction is hysterical:

> She was making a curious noise, a steady, repeated, low-pitched moan that sounded as if it came from the pit of her stomach, as if she'd been sick over and over again and still wanted to be sick. . . . When she felt that she was sitting on the bed next to him she threw herself forward so that her face was on his thigh. In a moment he felt moisture creeping through to his skin. He tried to lift her, but she was immovably heavy; her shoulders were shaking more rapidly than seemed to him normal even in a condition of this kind. Then she raised herself, tense but still trembling, and began a series of high-pitched, inward screams which alternated with the deep moans. Both were quite loud. Her hair was in her eyes, her lips were drawn back, and her teeth chattered. Her face was wet, with saliva as well as tears. At last, as he began speaking her name, she threw herself violently backwards and sideways on the bed. While she lay there with her arms spread out, writhing, she screamed half a dozen times, very loudly, then went on more quietly, moaning with every outward breath. . . .
> 'Hysterics, eh?' Atkinson said, and slapped Margaret several times on the face, very hard, Dixon thought. He pushed Dixon out of the way and sat down on the bed, gripping Margaret by the shoulders and shaking her vigorously. 'There's some whisky up in my cupboard. Go and get it.'
> Dixon ran out and up the stairs. The only thought that presented itself to him at all clearly was one of mild surprise that the fictional or cinematic treatment of hysterics should be based so firmly on what was evidently the right treatment.
> (From *Lucky Jim* (Victor Gollancz, London, 1953, p. 163))

The description of the fit of hysterics is pitilessly externalised and noticeably protracted. Jim's thought as he runs up the stairs emphasises the brutally circumstantial detail. The fictional portrayal of female hysterics, he notes, is remarkably accurate. The physical symptoms of hysteria are described with the authority of a medical encyclopedia. In this way the woman is subjected to a male gaze of knowing recognition: '"Hysterics, eh?", Atkinson said.' At the same time the hysteria is presented as strange: the defamiliarisation (see section 5) works to *objectify* the woman and to distance the reader from all empathy. The last thing Amis wants the reader to do is to sympathise with Margaret. He even implies that she is indulging in hysteria knowingly: 'When she felt that she was sitting on the bed next to him she threw herself forward so that her face was on his thigh.' Despite his recognition of the symptoms of hysteria at the end of the passage, Jim doesn't quite know what is going on at the time. From a feminist viewpoint we can see that this apparent contradiction has a clear motive. The initial puzzlement is part of a calculated objectivity in the description: 'Now and then she gave a quiet, almost skittish little scream. Her face was pushed hard against his chest. Dixon didn't know whether she was fainting, or having a fit of hysterics, or simply breaking down and crying.' What mysterious creatures women are; we find it so difficult to interpret them! The subsequent confirmation of the diagnosis has already been explained above. This means that the passage confirms two contradictory stereotypes:

1. Women are strange creatures.
2. Women are predictable creatures.

The physicality of the description of Margaret's hysteria has a further significance. As Mary Ellmann notes (in *Thinking about Women*), in gender stereotypes there is 'a repeated association of women with nature and of men with art'. Women are differentiated from men as creatures of nature: their concerns, their emotions and their needs are determined by their biological natures. Their 'strange' behaviour is caused by glandular secretions and bodily processes unknown to men. In this way the inexplicable in women is explained in terms of female biology: women are the helpless victims of their bodies. Significantly, the word 'hysteria' is derived from the Greek word for uterus (*hysteron*), which was thought by the Greeks to be the origin of specifically female diseases (in Renaissance English the word 'mother' also meant 'womb', as in 'fits of the mother'). One version of the Greek notion suggests that noxious vapours ascend from the uterus because of sexual abstinence. This explanation neatly fits the description of the jilted Margaret in *Lucky Jim*.

One might object that Jim is at least as much a victim of Amis's laughter as Margaret. He is shown to be incompetent, unable to grasp Margaret's condition and only able to talk knowingly about it after Atkinson has entered and dealt with the problem efficiently by slapping her face. Throughout the novel he is out of touch and unable to interpret signs. However, any comedy at Jim's expense is more than counterbalanced by the essentially male orientation of the entire narrative. The female characters are always the objects of male gaze, and only that. Both Margaret and Christine are in this sense 'sex objects': they exist as characters only as the focus of male attention. Margaret's failure in this role is her central characteristic: 'Margaret was talking again, animatedly; her face was a little flushed and her lipstick had been more carefully applied than usual. She looked as if she was enjoying herself; her sort of minimal prettiness was in evidence.' The harshness of a male gaze is evident here.

The central issue about this example from *Lucky Jim* cannot be resolved simply by asserting that Jim is a male chauvinist and therefore so is Amis. One has to show that the text is set up at a deeper level as a fiction of male desire or fantasy, that the narrative structure defines women as objects and not as subjects, and that the novel (consciously or unconsciously) builds its comedy upon the stereotyping of women as the unknown, all-too-familiar 'Other' (that which is defined only in terms of its difference from the male). It has often been noticed that comedy and laughter feed upon harsh female stereotypes (the mother-in-law, the dumb blond, the nagging wife). Even a novel as sophisticated as Amis's relies on such primitive drives and fantasies.

Section 21

Texts: Anne Bradstreet, 'The Author of Her Book', and Fleur Adcock, 'The Ex-Queen among the Astronomers'

Theory: Feminist Criticism (Writing as a Woman)

Is there a 'women's language'? Do women write differently from men as a result of biological, experiential or cultural differences? Women have different bodies, different physical experiences (childbirth, menstruation), different role models. Do these differences produce a distinctively gendered discourse?

It must be said immediately that the domination of literary culture by men has meant that, historically, many women have written within the constraints of patriarchy (literally the 'rule of the father'). They have aped the styles and followed the generic conventions of an essentially male culture. They have written anonymously or pseudonomously in order to conceal their gender. Only when a genre was recognised as a suitable vehicle for women's experience (the novel) did it become possible to succeed in writing as a woman, though if you wanted to write a novel of 'scope' and 'power' you still had to pretend to be a man (Mary Ann Evans became 'George Eliot', Emily Brontë became the indeterminate 'Ellis Bell'). It is difficult to calculate the effects of these constraints, but there is little doubt that women writers have suffered a number of disadvantages. Their education was subordinated to their brothers' (Virginia Woolf, despite her considerable learning, felt aggrieved at the denial of a formal education); their writings were often dismissed as limited and pretty; the alternative to being marginalised was to accept the dominant conventions of literary value and to allow their own concerns to be submerged.

What I have said so far implies that, given freedom and opportunity, women write differently. However, this is easier said than demonstrated. It is not difficult to see that women's writing will have a different viewpoint and a different content. However, is it possible to argue that women's handling of larger structures (plot, sequence) is less 'masculine'? It is even more difficult to show that women's discourse is different – that the phrases, sentences and paragraphs women produce are gendered in some sense. It is easier to describe the stereotyped characteristics of men's and women's writing as dictated by sexist conventions. The following typology emerges:

MALE: knowledge, power, clarity, conciseness, strong action
FEMALE: feeling, touch, domestic intimacy, small-scale forms, weak action

These assumptions are clearly *culturally derived* and cannot be assumed to have a biological foundation. It would be possible to provide many examples in support of this male/female dichotomy. However, all it would prove is that the culture of patriarchy has to some extent succeeded in imposing its will upon literature. One might argue that George Eliot adopted the characteristics of the male writer. This is true, except that she also injected a strong new direction in the novel towards a focus upon domestic intimacy. Nevertheless, it was virtually impossible to tell that the novelist was a woman. Experiments in blind gendering of literary texts have produced negative results: not only do women sometimes write like men, but also men can write like women.

Poststructuralist work on women's writing tends to confirm this anti-essentialist conclusion. Julia Kristeva, in 'The Semiotic and the Symbolic' (in *The Kristeva Reader*, 1986, pp. 89–136), links 'feminine' discourse with the pre-linguistic 'babble' of the child before it enters the 'symbolic' system of language (which she identifies with the 'father'). This childish 'language' of pure rhythm and intonation is the supposed foundation of a 'feminine' discourse which is suppressed by the advent of 'masculine' language proper (with its rigidities of syntax, denotation and closed meanings). Kristeva went on to show that this 'semiotic' phase (she uses the term *le sémiotique* in an unusual way) can be recovered, especially in avant-garde poetry and prose. The writings of Mallarmé and Joyce (in *Finnegans Wake*) show this recovery. The 'symbolic' system insists on fixed meanings, but in modernist writings meaning proliferates in a joyous rhythmical play of sound and free signification. What emerges from this is that 'feminine' and 'masculine' languages have little to do with a writer's gender. If language is gendered, then there are no biological boundaries preventing either sex from assuming a particular gendered form of discourse.

Anne Bradstreet (1612?–1672), the first important American poet, was born in England into a nonconformist family and settled in America after her marriage to Simon Bradstreet, who, like her father, was a prominent figure in the Massachusetts Bay Company. A book of her poems was published in London without her permission in 1650. The authorised edition was published in 1678 after her death. Her poems are, on the whole, written in the familiar styles of the second quarter of the seventeeth century. The style and form of her poems are in no sense gendered. She sometimes takes up a traditional form and turns it in a different direction. For example, in 'The Prologue' she regrets that her humble lines are poor substitutes for the great themes of martial epic. Before we jump to the wrong conclusion we should note that this is a topic of 'low' style genres. The Roman poet Horace, for example, apologises for his 'pedestrian muse' which cannot soar to the heights of epic verse. Nevertheless, there a distinctly female angle in her poem:

> Let Greeks be Greeks, and women what they are
> Men have precedency and still excel,
> It is but vain unjustly to wage war;
> Men can do best, and women know it well.
> Preeminence in all and each is yours;
> Yet grant some small acknowledgement of ours.
> (This and the following poem from *The Works*, ed. J. Hensley (Harvard University Press, Cambridge, Mass. and London, 1967, pp. 16 and 224))

This is truly submissive with no sense of irony: women cannot compete with men, and ask only recognition for their own small though inferior achievements. 'We know we can't rise to your level, but at least permit us to perform at our own level.' Nothing could show more clearly the sense of limitation felt by early women writers. Bradstreet's extreme humility as a writer speaks volumes. When we read a poem written out of a woman's experience, we find it difficult to separate out a specifically female *style of writing*. Here is Bradstreet's 'Before the Birth of One of Her Children' (addressed to her husband):

> All things within this fading world hath end,
> Adversity doth still our joys attend;
> No ties so strong, no friends so dear and sweet,
> But with death's parting blow is sure to meet. . .
> How soon, my Dear, death may my steps attend,
> How soon't may be thy lot to lose thy friend,
> We both are ignorant, yet love bids me
> These farewell lines to recommend to thee,
> That when that knot's untied that made us one,
> I may seem thine, who in effect am none.
> And if I see not half my days that's due
> What nature would, God grant to yours and you;

The many faults that well you know I have
Let be interred in my oblivious grave;
If any worth or virtue were in me,
Let that live freshly in thy memory . . .
And when thy loss shall be repaid with gains
Look to my little babes, my dear remains.
And if thou love thyself, or loved'st me,
These O protect from step-dames's injury.
And if chance to thine eyes shall bring this verse,
With some sad sighs honour my absent hearse;
And kiss this paper for thy love's dear sake,
Who with salt tears this last farewell did take.

It is a poem written by a wife to a husband, and by a mother concerned for her children. It bears all the marks of a subjected position in the family structure. It is distinctive of earlier women's experience: child-birth and death are inevitably associated. It is possible to say that even commonplace poetic topics received a gendered set of connotations in such poems. 'The fading world', and 'Adversity' take on a more alienated and fatalistic sense. The woman's humility is not unlike the religious humility of a man's poem, yet could any seventeenth-century man ever have written to his wife the lines 'If any worth or virtue were in me,/Let that live freshly in thy memory'? One could imagine the lines being written by a male poet of his good name: 'thy memory' would be addressed to the educated reader or to another man of high status. The phrase 'And when thy loss shall be repaid with gains' (taken with the reference to a possible 'step-dame') seems to allude discreetly to the inevitable remarriage of the husband (after all, the male line must be sustained). Leaving aside these marks of women's *experience* and subordination, there is nothing in Bradstreet's style, diction, prosody, or allusions which one could regard as gendered.

In modern poetry women writers are fond of turning the tables on men, of inverting the stereotypes, and of foregrounding women's experience without accepting a male valuation of that experience. In order to privilege women's experience or women's priorities, they must produce a recognisably feminine discourse. However, there is always a danger that the attempt to write as a woman will result in the apparent acceptance of sexist stereotypes. If 'feeling' or 'intuition' or 'the small-scale' are given prominence, the writer risks being consigned to a female ghetto – a safe sanctuary where women are permitted to let off steam and do their own thing. In this scenario men may still be seen to be setting the agenda. Some French feminist writings, for example Hélène Cixous' famous 'The laugh of the Medusa' (in *New French*

Feminisms, ed. Marks and de Courtivron, 1981, pp. 245–64), are open
to this charge. Their emphasis on the specificities of the female body –
writing '*concentric*' ('cunt-centric') as opposed to 'phallic' discourse –
threatens to produce a gender polarity which is hard to distinguish from
the male chauvinist version.

Fleur Adcock's 'The Ex-Queen among the Astronomers' is un-
doubtedly a poem written by a woman, but it avoids some of the
problems I have discussed:

> They serve revolving saucer eyes,
> dishes of stars; they wait upon
> huge lenses hung aloft to frame
> the slow procession of the skies.
>
> They calculate, adjust, record,
> watch transits, measure distances.
> They carry pocket telescopes
> to spy through when they walk abroad.
>
> Spectra possess their eyes; they face
> upwards, alert for meteorites,
> cherishing little glassy worlds:
> receptacles for outer space.
>
> But she, exiled, expelled, ex-queen,
> swishes among the men of science
> waiting for cloudy skies, for nights
> when constellations can't be seen.
>
> She wears the rings he let her keep;
> she walks as she was taught to walk
> for his approval, years ago.
> His bitter features taunt her sleep.
>
> And so when these have laid aside
> their telescopes, when lids are closed
> between machine and sky, she seeks
> terrestrial bodies to bestride.
>
> She plucks this one or that among
> the astronomers, and is become
> his canopy, his occultation;
> she sucks at earlobe, penis, tongue
>
> mouthing the tubes of flesh; her hair
> crackles, her eyes are comet-sparks.
> She brings the distant briefly close
> above his dreamy abstract stare.
>
> (From *Selected Poems* (Oxford University Press, Oxford, 1983))

Adcock uses various strategies to disorientate the (male) reader. For example, there appears to be an ironical allusion to the famous opening of George Herbert's 'Vanitie':

> The fleet Astronomer can bore,
> And thred the spheres with his quick-piercing mind:
> He views their stations, walks from door to door,
> Surveys, as if he had design'd
> To make a purchase there: he sees their dances,
> And knoweth long before
> Both their full-ey'd aspects, and secret glances.

In Herbert's poem the (male) astronomer has a 'quick-piercing mind', capable of seeing through the entire cosmic scene. In Adcock's poem the position of the men is immediately reversed: 'They *serve* revolving saucer eyes', and '*wait upon* huge lenses'. Herbert's astronomer sees 'their full-ey'd aspects', while Adcock's not only serve saucer eyes but have passive eyes ('Spectra *possess* their eyes'). Literary allusion is often a weapon of male authority – a sign of mastery over a predesignated field of knowledge. Adcock uses allusion to redefine the values upon which a tradition is built. Rather than tacitly drawing upon the values inherent in Herbert's poem she boldly turns them to feminist ends. Ironically her victim is the gentlest and most 'feminine' of all male English poets.

The astronomers' preoccupation with abstract science (calculating, measuring, recording) is ironically presented as if they were in the position of subjected females rather than masterful males. Their eyes are replaced by the mechanical eyes of modern technology which they serve passively. They 'serve', 'wait upon' and 'cherish' as if they were wives and mothers. They are mere 'receptacles' (a bitter reversal, with sexual undertones). Stanzas four and five introduce the 'ex-queen', at first seen as object of male neglect: she is waiting for a cloudy night when the men will have to stay at home. She wears women's clothes ('swishes'), walks for male eyes and keeps the jewellery her former partner gave her. Her dreams are dominated by his bitter face. In the last three stanzas the poem moves into another gear. Unexpectedly, the ex-queen is transformed into a creature of the flesh, whose active powers are in marked contrast to the men's passivity: she 'seeks . . . to bestride' (compare Shakespeare's Mark Antony: 'his legs bestrid the Ocean'); she 'plucks' (men usually 'pluck' the virginity of young maidens); she 'sucks'. Her domination of 'terrestrial bodies' contrasts with the men's subjection to the 'skies'. Her eyes parallel the meteorites for which the men search. Adcock conjures up potentially pornographic images in 'sucks at earlobe, penis, tongue/mouthing tubes of flesh', only to mock male fantasies of sexual domination; the female is the predator, and her vitality is cosmic in scale. In this passage Adcock plays with the imagery of metaphysical poetry which often used cosmic imagery to represent human love. The ex-queen asserts her authority over the male ('this one or that') by bringing him to earth, so to speak. She reminds him that 'tubes of flesh' are more in touch with reality than 'pocket telescopes'.

This poem refuses to conform to any received genre. Neither does it simply react to patriarchy by asserting a reversed order of female domination. After all, the queen has been dethroned, and her assertion of power is only 'brief'. The poem avoids finality and closure. It loosens up the patterns of the gender system, and questions the stereotypes which the male tradition perpetuates without merely inverting them. To displace the patriarchal patterns of meaning requires an indirectness and unpredictability which may make poems challenging and difficult rather than easily consumable.

The idea of a specifically 'women's language' is perhaps a mirage. A use of language which disrupts fixed subject positions (see section 10) is not necessarily a women's language, as Kristeva has shown. However, women writers have often brilliantly redirected and refashioned received genres and styles in order to achieve a true difference of view.

Section 22

Text: Daniel Defoe, *Moll Flanders*

Theory: Marxist Criticism (Literature and Ideology)

In ordinary usage 'ideology' usually means 'political doctrine', 'system of ideas', or, more generally, 'way of thinking'. Marxists use 'ideology' as a comprehensive term to cover social consciousness in general including such areas as religion, education, the law, the economy, social relations and culture. Ideology is the total system of such ideas. Marxists argue that ideology always represents the values of a particular social class, and is based on its economic interests. For example, 'bourgeois ideology' refers to the entire constellation of ideological practices which were historically developed as the consciousness of the bourgeois class. In so far as the middle classes, which make up the bourgeoisie, have come to dominate society (the date varies from country to country), their ideology has also achieved dominance.

In recent years Marxists have refined the notion of ideology. An influential definition was propounded by the French Marxist Louis Althusser who conceives ideology as the *imaginary* ways in which people *represent* to themselves their *real relationship to the world* (see 'Ideology and Ideological State Apparatuses' in *Lenin and Philosophy and Other Essays*, 1971, pp. 123–73). So, ideology does not refer to 'theories', or 'political ideas', or any kind of consciously formulated propositions about society. Althusser believes that ideology is like the air we breathe and is the seemingly natural discourse which makes possible our sense of existence as human 'subjects' (socially and psychologically). Ideology is closely related to what we call 'common sense'. Althusser's views differ from earlier Marxist thinkers, who believed that ideology was a kind of 'false consciousness' produced by capitalism, which could be dispelled by scientific knowledge. Althusser, who also believes that only Marxism possesses a 'scientific' knowledge of ideology, nevertheless shows that we cannot avoid working with some imaginary representations which help us to make sense of social experience. The State Apparatuses (religious, cultural, educational, judicial, and so on) help to sustain the dominant ideology and to reproduce it by situating human subjects as 'subjects of ideology'. This is done by a process Althusser calls 'interpellation' (hailing). All subjects are greeted by the discourse of a particular State Apparatus: it summons them into their places (as occurs, for example, when believers hear Christ calling them to follow Him). This account of how dominant ideologies reproduce their dominance leaves out the dimension of resistance: we also need to know how emergent classes and ideologies become dominant. However, a newly emergent ideology works in the same manner (through interpellation) as the ideological discourses it supplants.

How does the Marxist theory of ideology account for literature? First, it is important to note that some Marxist explanations of literature's relationship with ideology are highly 'reductive': they treat literary texts as the direct expression of the writer's ideology or of the class whom the writer represents. Engels' discussion of Balzac's realism, in a letter to Margaret Harkness (April 1888, in Marx and Engels, *On Literature and Art*, ed. Baxandall and Morawski, 1974, pp. 115–17), rejects such reductivism. He shows that Balzac's novels give a remarkably accurate and dispassionate account of the rise of the bourgeoisie in French society, despite the fact that he was a deeply-committed royalist. It seems that ideology may be represented in literature at a 'subconscious' level. Althusser developed this insight by showing that major literature gives us a sense of what it is like to exist within a particular ideology, and produces this sense of 'lived' ideology because *literary form* is capable of showing us the nature of ideology with a sort of *aesthetic detachment*. Subsequently, critics of Althusser have suggested that in making literature superior to ideology he destroys the fundamental Marxist subordination of culture to social structure. Taking a larger historical view, Marxist critics often argue that literary forms (as opposed to writers or even specific works) are themselves expressions of class ideologies. For example, the novel can be seen to have revealed *in its very form* a new set of social priorities (those of the middle classes): its emphasis upon the life-like representation of the material lives of 'rounded' individuals is the very substance of bourgeois ideology from a Marxist viewpoint. In selecting a form in which to work a writer is already in a sense ideologically circumscribed.

Pierre Macherey, whose *A Theory of Literary Production* (1966) influenced Althusser's views, introduced the idea that literary form was capable not merely of telling us something about ideology but of transforming ideology into 'fiction' and thereby of showing us its *internal incoherences and contradictions*. Ideology's 'imaginary' representations of reality have a specious coherence made possible only by the repression of unconscious contradictions and by whole areas of silent omission. By 'producing' an ideology in the form of a fiction the writer makes us feel these gaps, silences and absences which in their purely ideological form are less apparent. I would compare this effect with the common human experience of trying to write down in actual words thoughts which appear perfectly coherent in the mind. Such purely mental thoughts often fail to cohere in written form and reveal omissions, lapses and incoherences. In the same way a literary text, according to Macherey, can show the incoherence of ideology. The presence of ideology in the text is apparent in the silences and contradictions which the text is driven to reveal by the very nature of the ideology it works upon.

These ideas are easier to grasp if we apply them. Daniel Defoe's *Moll Flanders* (1722) has been the subject of much debate by critics and historians. Marxists have considered Defoe's writings, especially *Moll Flanders* and *Robinson Crusoe*, to be expressions of bourgeois ideology. We have already pointed out that the novel form itself, which Defoe did much to develop, is, from a Marxist viewpoint, deeply ideological as a literary structure, and acts specifically as a vehicle of bourgeois ideology. A further important factor in our understanding of the novel's ideological bearings is the well-known argument, embodied in the famous 'Weber thesis', about the intimate connections between capitalism and the 'Protestant ethic'. Weber argued that the 'ascetic puritanism' of the seventeenth century was an important impulse behind the development of the modern 'spirit of capitalism' (his book *The Protestant Ethic and the Spirit of Capitalism* was published in 1930). Weber believed that Calvinistic Puritanism and the spirit of capitalism had a number of things in common. They included:

1. A vocational ethic ('calling') of religion and of work.
2. An 'ascetic' spirit which rejects immediate gratification in favour of long-term benefits.
3. An emphasis on rationality and calculation.

Calvin's particular 'inward' ethical attitude, which saw the individual life as a 'labour' for a deferred end, also resembled capitalist ideology. A

Marxist would see the development of this type of religious ideology as a symptom of capitalist development rather than as a cause of it.

Defoe himself for much of his life was both an entrepreneur and a religious dissenter. There has been some debate about the precise applicability of the Weber thesis to his personal life, but the relevance of the Puritan/capitalist ideological *mélange* to his novels is hard to deny. Moll, who tells her own story in the first person, is a successful thief and prostitute – an unlikely focus of Puritan values! However, the main justification for the narrative of her life of sin is the religious and moral lessons it affords. Throughout the novel we find a double perspective: Moll at times fully enters into the narration of her 'wicked' life, and at others stands back to lament her wicked ways. The effect appears somewhat schizophrenic. However, if we keep in mind the very close connections established by Weber between Puritan spiritual values and the calculating and profit-centred vocation of the entre-preneur, the double perspective appears less strange. The emergent middle-class ideology is a specific conflation of religious and secular discourses. The incoherences and contradictions are suppressed in the ideology's 'imaginary' representations.

It has often struck readers as odd that Moll can be so honest about her own shortcomings and yet, at the end of the story, can be so apparently without self-knowledge, when, after her period of imprison-ment in Newgate, she and her Lancashire husband settle in America. In order to set them up in business she uses a stock of capital accumulated from their profit in prostitution, shop-lifting, housebreak-ing, pickpocketing and armed robbery. She easily overcomes her conscience and discovers a complacent satisfaction in her new-found respectability and good business prospects. When she returns to London on a visit, we read:

> I gave my Governess a History of my Travels; she lik'd the *Harwich* Journey well enough, and in Discoursing of these things between ourselves she observ'd, that a Thief being a Creature that Watches the Advantages of other People's mistakes, 'tis possible but that to one that is vigilant and industrious many Opportunities must happen, and therefore she thought that one so exquisitely keen in the Trade as I was, would scare fail of something extraordinary wherever I went.
>
> On the other hand, every Branch of my Story, if duly consider'd, may be useful to honest People, and afford a due Caution to People of some sort or other to Guard against the like Surprizes, and to have their Eyes about them when they have to do with Strangers of any kind, for 'tis very seldom that some Snare or other is not in their way. The Moral indeed of all my History is left to be gather'd by the Senses and Judgement of the Reader; I

am not Qualified to preach to them. Let the Experience of one Creature completely Wicked, and completely Miserable, be a Storehouse of useful warning to those that read.
(From *Moll Flanders*, ed. Edward Kelly (W. W. Norton, New York, 1973, pp. 209–10))

First, we notice that theft is described in terms of a business ethic: 'vigilant and industrious', 'keen in the trade'. A successful thief needs to have the same outlook as a successful entrepreneur: ruthless opportunism and hard work. Like Gay's *Beggar's Opera*, written at about the same time, *Moll Flanders* suggests that the new and ruthless capitalists of the times resemble in their values the criminal underworld of the day. Secondly, Moll sees her criminal life as a perfect lesson (a 'Storehouse of useful warning') for the pious reader. The paradoxical and contradictory nature of the text is not, as some have suggested, a sign of Defoe's lack of artistry, but a direct effect of the ideology which Defoe 'produces' in his text. The literary form – especially the use of retrospective narration – works upon the ideological material of Puritan and entrepreneurial discourse, and reveals the sewn-together and ramshackle nature of ideology. Looking back on her life Moll moralises piously, but at the same time she cannot help conveying a sense of the forward movement of her earlier life of 'crime', a movement which at times has a strongly entrepreneurial relish.

At their best, Marxist studies of literature and ideology (see, for example, Jonathan Dollimore's *Radical Tragedy*, 1984) create a sense of critical liberation. The reader is able to escape the stifling rigidities of formalism or Romantic individualism, and to understand texts as complex reworkings of socially marked discourses. No longer is it necessary to evaluate the literary work as an expression of personal genius. Instead, the reader can engage in a delicate study of the artistic transformation of ideological representations.

Section 23

Text: James Joyce, *Ulysses*
Theory: Marxism and Modernism (Georg Lukács and Bertolt Brecht)

The Marxist tradition has always faced a problem arising from the fact that the dominant traditions of writing since the eighteenth century have been middle-class. This has predisposed some Marxists (including Marx and Engels themselves) to look for 'progressive' aspects of bourgeois writing rather than merely to damn all pre-socialist culture as reactionary. There is some irony in the fact that the orthodox Soviet socialist realism of the 1930s treated nineteenth-century bourgeois fiction as a formal model but considered the anti-bourgeois writings of modernist authors to be decadent and reactionary.

During the 1930s two major figures of the Marxist tradition adopted opposing views of the nature of realism, socialist literature and modernist experimental writing. The Brecht–Lukács debate (it is called a 'debate', but was not consciously conducted as one at the time) remains of interest today because it anticipates later critical controversies about the nature of representation and of the relations between literature and society (See Henri Arvon, *Marxist Aesthetics*, 1973, chapter 7). Since the rise of poststructuralism, Althusser, Macherey, Eagleton and Jameson have reworked the Marxist heritage in order to redefine it in a postmodern form. From this perspective the drama and theory of Brecht prefigure a break with the scientific and humanistic attitudes of the pre-structuralist age. Brecht and Lukács disagreed about the way in which art and literature should represent the world of late capitalism. The broad and European-wide movement known as Modernism (c. 1890–1930) included various sub-movements (symbolism, imagism, futurism, expressionism, surrealism and so on), all of which challenged the realistic and romantic writings of the nineteenth century. Modernists questioned confident assumptions about reason and progress, and rejected the possibility of human mastery of the world, retreating into inner experience and into mythic or psychological themes. Lukács reacted strongly against the formal devices exploited by modernist writers; their abandonment of a unified perspective and their resort to techniques of disruption (montage, collage, multiple perspectives, reportage, episodic structure, and so on) reflected, he believed, the alienation and fragmentation of human existence in late capitalist society, threatened as it was by fascism and imperialism. Brecht's attitude to the experiments of expressionists and surrealists was quite different; in his view socialist artists had to make use of every possible device which might assist the process of *changing* an unjust society.

Lukács thought that the novel, a bourgeois literary form, had, by the early nineteenth century, recovered some of the concreteness and harmony of the classical Greek epic. For example, he considered that novels give a rounded and intensive 'reflection' of the rising bourgeoisie and a sense of the individual's interaction with the whole structure of society. Lukács regarded the bourgeois novel as the ideal form for 'realistic' representation of social development. Socialist realism required new content, but not new forms. He attacked modernism for its subjectivity, pessimism and formalism. By 'formalism' he meant its preoccupation with formal experiment as an end in itself.

Brecht's 'epic' theatre embraced new technical devices, sometimes borrowed from contemporary modernists and sometimes from other cultures, in order to *disrupt* the audience's complacent acceptance of their world. The 'alienation effects' in his plays aimed to prevent the audience from passively identifying with the characters and treating them as universal and unproblematic. He wanted people not to sink back on a wave of sympathetic emotion, but to criticise the social order by responding to the questions raised in his plays, and to develop an intellectual basis for political action. His approach to literary form is uncompromisingly *political*: his concern was with *changing* the world, and not with merely understanding it. Lukács' admiration extended to those novels which, regardless of their authors' political commitments, produced a historical understanding of society. Brecht regarded Lukács' commitment to the nineteenth-century novel as a kind of 'formalism' – a belief that only one form had the historical mission to comprehend bourgeois society. Brecht was not interested in knowledge and understanding for their own sakes; he valued only art's ability to transform people's *political* consciousness.

Lukács argued that the twin enemies of realism were 'naturalism' and 'expressionism'; the former dominated late nineteenth-century, the latter early twentieth-century literature. Naturalism was one-sided in its obsession with the external appearances of things, while expressionism and other modernist movements were one-sided in their obsession with internal and subjective experiences. 'Realism', he contended, must bring the external and internal into 'spontaneous' unity. He saw hope in the new bourgeois democratic writers, such as Thomas Mann, who preserved the totalising power of the nineteenth-century novel, but he condemned Dos Passos, Proust, Kafka and Joyce as decadent formalists (see especially 'The Ideology of Modernism', in *The Meaning of Contemporary Realism*, 1962). Joyce's *Ulysses* seemed to him a powerful artistic performance, but one in which 'perpetually oscillating patterns of sense- and memory-data ... give rise to an epic structure which is *static* reflecting a belief in the basically static character of events.' His objection is to the world-view implied in the novel, but he also thought that its undynamic and pessimistic conception of human history inevitably produced stylistic devices which expressed a similarly fragmented and alienated perspective.

Consider the following passage from the episode in the library in which Stephen Dedalus (Joyce's *alter ego*) discusses *Hamlet* with other Irish critics:

– As we ... weave and unweave our bodies, Stephen said, from day to day, their molecules shuttled to and fro, so does the artist weave and unweave his image. And as the mole on my right breast is where it was when I was born, though all my body has been woven of new stuff time after time, so through the ghost of the unquiet father the image of the unliving son looks forth. In the intense instant of imagination, when the mind, Shelley says, is a fading coal, that which I was is that which I am and that which in possibility I may come to be. So in the future, the sister of the past, I may see myself as I sit here now but by reflection from that which then I shall be.

Drummond of Hawthorden helped you at that stile.

– Yes, Mr Best said youngly, I feel Hamlet quite young. The bitterness might be from the father but the passages with Ophelia are surely from the son.

Has the wrong sow by the lug. He is in my father. I am in his son.

– That mole is the last to go, Stephen said, laughing.

John Eglinton made a nothing pleasing mow.

– If that were the birthmark of genius, he said, genius would be a drug in the market. The plays of Shakespeare's later years which Renan admired so much breathe another spirit.

– The spirit of reconciliation, the quaker librarian breathed.

– There can be no reconciliation, Stephen said, if there has not been a sundering.

Said that.
– If you want to know what are the events which cast their shadow over
the hell of time of *King Lear*, *Othello*, *Hamlet*, *Troilus and Cressida*, look to
see when and how the shadow lifts. What softens the heart of a man,
Shipwrecked in storms dire, Tried, like another Ulysses, Pericles, prince
of Tyre?
Head, redconecapped, buffeted, brineblinded.
– A child, a girl placed in his arms, Marina.
(From *Ulysses* (Bodley Head, London, 1960, pp. 249–50))

Stephen, whose aesthetic education is charted in *Portrait of the Artist as
a Young Man*, is the spiritual son of Leopold Bloom, who is the Ulysses
of Homer's epic to Stephen's Telemachus (Ulysses' son). The effect of
the elaborate correspondences between Homer's world and Joyce's
Dublin has been much debated, but it can be said that they are part of a
complex web of such paradigmatic patterns, linking (often ironically)
the concrete world of Dublin and the entire cultural history of the
world. Lukács would see the mythic dimension of the novel as evidence
of its static, non-developmental view of human history. A single day in
1904 becomes the epitome of all human history. The trivial and
everyday events of Dublin life are overlaid with an infinite series of
parallels and ironic contrasts. John Fletcher and Malcolm Bradbury
tend to confirm Lukács' view of such modernist work when they write:

> Parody and pastiche, the use of plurality of language, demonstrate the lack
> of plot and discourse in the contemporary world. The novel contains the
> degenerate history which the symbol must transcend; the compulsion
> towards technique becomes a feature of a world in which there is no
> coherence to give outside the coherence of art. (In *Modernism 1890–1930*
> (eds Malcolm Bradbury and James McFarlane), 1976, pp. 405–6)

The passage presents an aspect of Stephen's aesthetic view of
existence. The patterns of Shakespeare's plays are the patterns of
human life. They are repeated in cyclical fashion, just as the wandering
Ulysses is repeated in Pericles, Prospero and Bloom, the lost child in
Perdita and Marina, the searching son in Telemachus, Hamlet and
Stephen Dedalus. History is seen as an endlessly recurring set of
symbols and images (of 'topoi' – recurring motifs). Everything changes,
and yet everything is the same. Hamlet's father – the ghost – is
Shakespeare and Hamlet is Hamnet (Shakespeare's dead son): 'through
the ghost of the unquiet father the image of the unliving son looks
forth'. Stephen draws upon the entire European tradition (including
Shelley here) in his endeavour to express his view of art. The central
concept is the 'symbol', the artistic image which survives time and gives

meaning to life. Joyce's fondness for word-play is only modestly displayed in the extract. For example, the 'mole' on Stephen's breast is associated with old Hamlet (Hamlet calls him 'old mole' when he cries out under the stage), and then undergoes a further metaphoric translation in 'the birthmark of genius'. Note also the pun on 'stile'. Joyce's stylistic exuberance is present in the entire library chapter in the form of a parody of academic literary English of the period. 'John Eglington made a nothing pleasing mow' is in mock Shakespearean idiom.

A Lukácsian critic would regard the aestheticism, the foregrounding of style, the preoccupation with subjective and psychological experience and especially the symbolist view of time and history as symptomatic of the alienation of the individual in a society in which objective reality is reduced to the impersonal processes of the market. The fragmentation of social existence is more strikingly evoked by Bloom's interior monologues in the Dublin streets. Raymond Williams, whose work shares common themes with Lukács, admires the novel and yet characterises it in a remarkably Lukácsian manner:

> The genius of *Ulysses* is that it dramatizes three minds – Bloom, Stephen and Molly – and their interaction is the necessary tension. But what each enacts for the other is a symbolic role, and the reality to which they must ultimately relate is no longer a place and a time, for all the anxious dating of that day in Dublin. It is an abstracted or more strictly an imposed pattern of man and woman, father and son; a family but not a family, out of touch and searching for each other through a myth and a history. (*The English Novel from Dickens to Lawrence*, 1974, pp. 135–6)

It is possible to turn Lukács on his head and to regard this drama of isolated consciousnesses positively as a powerful image of modern society rather than as an unconscious symptom of alienation. Brecht believed that writers must exploit new formal devices in order to capture the elusive flow of reality. The old forms will not continue to represent 'the real' as they once did. This does not mean that Brecht accepted the ideological implications of formal devices in modernist writers, but he did not accept Lukács' view that the modernist revolution was of no use to the socialist writer. Brecht has more in common with Walter Benjamin and the Frankfurt School of Marxism, especially in their rejection of simplistic notions of reflection. Brecht realised that there was no simple equation between literary forms and the ideal of realism: the same text can be realist one day and anti-realist the next. The experiments of modernists should not be condemned as irretrievably decadent; the devices of reportage, montage, back projection, stream of consciousness, parody, alienation effect, all offer the socialist writer new ways of 'reflecting' the ever-changing reality of society. The fragmenting of consciousness and the dissolution of unified perspectives are valuable formal resources which can be used by writers such as Brecht to produce effective 'representations' of modern society.

Section 24

Texts: William Shakespeare, *King Lear* and *Twelfth Night*
Theory: Marxist Criticism (Literature and Class Struggle, and Bakhtin on Carnival)

In this chapter we will examine a passage from *King Lear* from two related but different viewpoints. The first is explicitly Marxist and concerns the reflection in the play of actual class conflict in early seventeenth-century England. The second, based on the theories of Mikhail Bakhtin, is also 'sociological' but at the same time focuses upon the ideological inflection of *language* (Bakhtin is sometimes discussed as a Marxist and sometimes as a reformed Russian Formalist).

Shakespeare's tragedies have often been regarded as near-sacred texts which embody a profound understanding of the 'human condition'. They have been valued as having *universal* application. Dr Johnson, the eighteenth-century critic, emphasised the general human truth of the plays. He did not deny the individuality of Shakespeare's characters but insisted that we ignore the historical details of the plays and concentrate upon the 'common humanity' of the characters who 'act and speak by the influence of those general passions and principles by which all minds are agitated, and the whole system of life is continued in motion'. By subordinating history to 'general passions' Johnson effectively suppresses the connections between Shakespeare's plays and the ideological and economic struggles and conflicts of his period.

Most Marxist accounts of social and economic developments in the early seventeenth century (see, for example, Christopher Hill, *The Century of Revolution 1603–1714*, Part 1, 1961) perceive two main features of conflict underlying the political, ideological and cultural life of England:

1. The gradual rise of middle-class entrepreneurs and the steady decline of the older 'feudal' ruling class.
2. The growth of a dispossessed mass of day-labourers and able-

bodied vagrants, accompanied by a steady increase in 'capitalist' agriculture and the 'enclosure' of the common lands.

If we look at *King Lear* in these terms, we see that the division between the main protagonists fits the first category of conflict: Lear, Gloucester and Kent represent the old feudal order with its values of 'hospitality' (generosity and abundant entertainment of rich and poor), duty, social hierarchy and honour; the 'bad' characters, Goneril, Regan and Edmund, represent the rising new class of grasping and ruthless individualists and, by extension, the economic forces of capitalism. It should be added that the aristocracy itself included older (feudal) and newer (progressive) sections. The former scorned the idea of 'business', but the latter were committed to speculation and enterprise in the interests of better estate management. Looked at in this light the play represents two contradictory tendencies within the same class. The second category of conflict concerns the theme of poverty and vagrancy which is prominent in several parts of the play: we enter a social world in which there are many wandering beggars and vagrants (see my 'King Lear and "True Need"', 1987). This had always been the case in England since the Middle Ages, but it was particularly true of the period between 1590 and 1610. Famine, enclosure and the decline of 'hospitality' all contributed to the problem. It is difficult for historians to assess the precise extent of homelessness and unemployment in the period, but certainly the authorities (secular and religious) were acutely conscious of an existing problem.

During and after the storm scenes in the play King Lear passes through a period of madness, in which he shares a hovel with Poor Tom (the disguised and exiled Edgar) and the Fool. He begins to realise how much the poor suffer and he laments the state's injustice. In his deranged conversation with the blind Gloucester he attacks people in authority:

> A man may see how this world goes with no eyes. Look with thine ears: see how yond justice rails upon yond simple thief. Hark, in thine ear: change places, and, handy-dandy, which is the justice, which is the thief? Thou has seen a farmer's dog bark at a beggar?
>
> Gloucester. Ay, Sir.
> Lear.   And the creature run from the cur? There thou might'st behold
>   The great image of Authority:
>   A dog's obey'd in office.
>   Thou rascal beadle, hold thy bloody hand!

> Why dost thou lash that whore? Strip thine own back;
> Thou hotly lusts to use her in that kind
> For which thou whipp'st her. The usurer hangs the cozener.
> Thorough tatter'd clothes small vices do appear;
> Robes and furr'd gowns hide all. Plate sin with gold,
> And the strong lance of justice hurtless breaks;
> Arm it in rags, a pigmy's straw does pierce it.
>
> (IV.vi.151–69)

A narrowly humanistic reading of this passage (following the approach of Dr Johnson or later humanist critics) might concentrate only upon the *general* truths uttered by the mad Lear, picking up Edgar's aside – 'Reason in madness'. However, a Marxist reading might look for connections between the injustices attacked by Lear and those of Shakespeare's own time. The heartless treatment of petty criminals is well documented in Shakespeare's period. Poor Tom, in Act III Scene iv, refers to the brutal treatment of vagrants who were 'whipp'd from tithing [the parish where they turned up] to tithing [their parish of origin], stock-punish'd, and imprison'd'. The passage alludes to the statute of 1597 which specified this punishment. A recurrence of bad behaviour of this kind (wandering) could result in execution. Lear declares that what determines the outcome of the judicial process is not the crime but the wealth or poverty of the criminal. In a period when many were thrown off their smallholdings or made redundant by their masters, vagrancy posed a serious threat to good order. The repressiveness of the authorities was felt especially by the landless and by homeless petty criminals. In *As You Like It* even the son of a gentleman is faced with the prospect of a life of crime. The faithful Adam tells Orlando to flee his brother Oliver. Orlando is dismayed as much by his loss of the means to live as by his brother's wickedness: 'wouldst thou have me go and beg my food,/Or with a base and boist'rous sword enforce/A thievish living on the common road?'

This historical focus raises difficult but important questions about Shakespeare's attitude to social injustice in his day. Are we to assume that Lear's outburst represents a genuine piece of social criticism? Does Lear speak for Shakespeare? If so, why does the theme disappear from the play after the mad scenes? One possible answer is that the injustice of his society was something which Shakespeare could not deal with, partly because he was committed to the existing social order and partly because he could not see a solution. All he could do was to register the problem in the heart of the play.

Some Marxists would now reject this type of approach for its 'mimetic' perspective; the influence of structuralism has convinced many Marxist critics that we cannot treat a literary text as a *reflection* of historical reality, because language cannot mirror the world but can only 'construct' it (on structuralism see sections 6–9). Much modern Marxist criticism is concerned with literature as part of ideological discourse (see section 22). From this point of view literature does not reflect but rather produces a discourse which shapes and reshapes available signifying practices.

The work of Mikhail Bakhtin provides a very different 'sociological' perspective. One of his central concepts is 'Carnival' which he believes to have particular importance for Renaissance literary studies (see his *Rabelais and his World*, 1968; for a short account of carnivalisation see *Problems of Dostoevsky's Poetics*, 1973, pp. 100–49). The festivities of popular culture (including the pre-Lent carnivals and the celebrations associated with marriages, midsummer and Christmas) promoted values which we are inclined to regard as completely outside recorded culture. However, Bakhtin shows that certain features of Carnival survive and inform high culture. Carnival is *collective* in feeling and popular, reflecting values which ruling-class ideology tends to ignore or patronise. An essential feature is the reversal of all hierarchies and conventional attitudes. Hierarchies are turned on their heads – fools become wise, kings become beggars; separate spheres are flung together – fact and fantasy, heaven and hell, spirit and body, life and death, are all confused. Everything which asserts authority, everthing fixed, rigid or serious, is mocked and treated with insulting and violent abuse. Bakhtin uses the term 'carnivalisation' to describe the transformation of literature by Carnival.

Carnivalisation is often comic and vulgar, but it can also be present in tragedy. The most obvious carnivalistic aspect of *King Lear* is the reversal of roles affecting Lear and the Fool. Lear, neglected by his two wicked daughters, is reduced to childish impotence and to literal beggary, while the Fool becomes his adviser and critic. The Fool declares to Lear 'I am better than thou art now; I am a Fool, thou art nothing' (I.iv.201–2). The Fool talks in riddles, mocks and insults his master and the rulers of the state. His discourse is full of carnivalistic disrespect and questioning of authority. Lear's ravings about judges, beadles and magistrates similarly depict a world turned upside-down. The fixed positions in the social hierarchy are mixed up and indistinguishable: 'Change places, and, handy-dandy, which is the justice, which is the thief?' 'Handy-dandy' alludes to the game in which one guesses in which hand an object is lying after it has been switched an arbitrary number of times from hand to hand. This evokes the spirit of Carnival, which shuffles all the cards of social position and lets them come out any way up they like. Carnival is profoundly egalitarian: kings and beggars are on a par. The clash between the unruly spirit of Carnival and the niggardly spirit of Lent underlies the conflict between Lear and his wicked daughters. They deny him the retinue he requires to maintain his old-style hospitality which is a ruling-class way of allowing Carnival its own space. Goneril (in Act I, Scene iv) complains of Lear's 'insolent retinue' who break 'forth/In rank and not-to-be-endured riots'. Lear 'should be wise'. His knights and squires are, in Goneril's view, 'so disorder'd, so debosh'd, and bold/That this our court. . ./Shows like a riotous inn.' Festivity is cut short by the mean-spirited Lenten daughter but resurfaces in Lear's mad outbursts and his contempt for ruling-class justice.

As a coda to this section we will glance at a comic form of carnivalised Shakespearian drama – the clash between Sir Toby Belch and Malvolio in *Twelfth Night*. The play's title alludes to what was originally part of the Christmas festivities. Sir Toby represents the pure spirit of Carnival bent on mocking the narrow and life-denying face of Lent as represented by the 'Puritan' Malvolio. Here is part of the famous scene in which Malvolio comes upon Sir Toby, Sir Andrew Aguecheek and Maria enjoying a drunken revel:

> *Malvolio.* My masters, are you mad? Or what are you? Have you no wit, manners, nor honesty, but to gabble like tinkers at this time of night? Do ye make an ale-house of my lady's house. . . ?
> *Sir Toby.* . . . Ye lie. Art any more than a steward? Dost thou think, because thou art virtuous, there shall be no more cakes and ale?

Toby's riotousness and Malvolio's disapproval are a typical embodiment of the conflict between Carnival and Lent. We notice that Malvolio's reaction to festivity is precisely the same as Goneril's ('this our court . . . Shows like a riotous inn'). Toby displays a flagrant disrespect for convention, middle-class 'virtue' and the moral restraint imposed from above. In this he shares the plebeian (common people's) refusal to accept the 'civilized' social order imposed by ruling élites of all kinds, a refusal expressed in popular festivities and holidays when the collective life of the people bubbles up and temporarily turns the world upside down. A conventional view of Toby's commitment to a life of 'cakes and ale' might suggest that the common people's culture is escapist, self-indulgent and coarse. This Lenten attitude has afflicted many critics in the past. The emphasis upon Carnival is not so much an indulgent attitude as a view 'from below' of the ruling class's severe and repressive moral and social attitudes. Carnivalised literature preserves something of this almost invisible counter-culture.

The two approaches we have considered in this section offer different ways of recovering the social roots of art. Bakhtin's writings have appealed strongly to those critics who are looking for ways of recovering the radical and popular elements in high culture which have been ignored or treated patronisingly by earlier critics. We should not leave this subject without noting that C. L. Barber (in *Shakespeare's Festive Comedy*, 1959) and several New Historicists (see section 13) do not believe that Carnival ever achieved true subversion because it was always contained by the aristocracy. Indeed, they argue, popular entertainments were positively encouraged (for example in King James's *Book of Sports*) as a convenient safety valve for social pressures. Seen in this light the clash we discussed between Toby and Malvolio neatly deflects the dangerous threat of Puritanism away from ruling-class values towards the hedonism of the people. Whichever view of the matter we take, we cannot but notice the radical change of focus which this type of sociological and historical criticism affords when compared with traditional Bradleian or formalistic studies of Shakespeare.

Exercises

The following exercises are intended to provide an opportunity for you to consolidate your understanding of the preceding chapters by applying modern critical concepts and methods to short poems and extracts from plays and novels. I have included questions which raise a number of issues about the individual passages from various critical angles. However, the questions are not exhaustive and you may wish to explore the passages from alternative viewpoints, including some not covered in this book.

EXERCISE 1

Think carefully about the steps of comprehension taken when you read
this opening section of Doris Lessing's Memoirs of a Survivor. How do
you interpret 'that time' (sentence 1)? What alterations in your
'actualisation' of the narrative occur as your reading proceeds? What
ways are there of interpreting 'before the end'? Is the uncertainty about
the narrative's direction annoying or fascinating or gripping? The
experiences described seem to be both bizarre and at the same time
common. What strategies for making sense of this contradiction can
you come up with (see sections 4, 5, 15–18)?

Describe the narrative technique used in the passage. Do you see any
evidence for thinking that the narrator is 'reliable' or 'unreliable' (see
sections 3 and 8)?

Use Barthes' 'codes' to open up meanings in the text and to produce
signifieds. Is it a 'plural text'? Does the answer to this question depend
on the reader or the text (see sections 10 and 16)?

We all remember that time. It was no different for me than for others. Yet
we do tell each other over and over again the particularities of the events
we shared, and the repetition, the listening, is as if we are saying: 'It was
like that for you, too? Then that confirms it, yes, it was so, it must have
been, I wasn't imagining things.' We match or dispute like people who
have seen remarkable creatures on a journey: 'Did you see that big blue
fish? Oh, the one you saw was yellow!' But the sea we travelled over was
the same, the protracted period of unease and tension before the end was
the same for everybody, everywhere; in the smaller units of our cities –
streets, a cluster of tall blocks of flats, a hotel, as in cities, nations, a
continent . . . yes, I agree that this is pretty highflown imagery considering
the nature of events in question: bizarre fish, oceans, and so forth. But
perhaps it wouldn't be out of place here to comment on the way we –
everyone – will look back over a period in life, over a sequence of events,
and find much more there than they did at the time. This is true even of
events as dispiriting as the litter left on a common after a public holiday.
People will compare notes, as if wishing or hoping for confirmation of
something the events themselves had not licensed – far from it, something
they had seemed to exclude altogether. Happiness? That's a word I have
taken up from time to time in my life, looked at – but I never did find that
it held its shape. A meaning, then; a purpose? At any rate, the past,
looked back on in this frame of mind, seems steeped in a substance that
had seemed foreign to it, was extraneous to the experiencing of it. Is it
possible that this is the stuff of real memory? Nostalgia, no; I'm not talking
of that, the craving, the regret – not that poisoned itch. Nor is it a
question of the importance each one of us tries to add to our not very
significant pasts: 'I was there, you know. I saw that.'

But it is because of this propensity of ours that perhaps I may be permitted the fancy metaphors. I *did* see fish in that sea, as if whales and dolphins had chosen to show themselves coloured scarlet and green, but did not understand at the time what it was I was seeing, and certainly did not know how much my own personal experience was common, was shared: this is what, looking back, we acknowledge first – our similarities, not our differences.

One of the things we now know was true for everybody, but which each of us privately thought was evidence of a stubbornly preserved originality of mind, was that we apprehended what was going on in ways that were not official. Not respectable. Newscasts and newspapers and pronouncements were what we were used to, what we by no means despised: without them we would have become despondent, anxious, for of course one must have the stamp of the official, particularly in a time when nothing is going according to expectation. But the truth was that every one of us became aware at some point that it was not from official sources we were getting the facts which were building up into a very different picture from the publicized one. Sequences of words were crystallizing events into a picture, almost a story: *And then this happened, and so-and-so said* . . . but more and more often these were words dropped during a casual conversation, and perhaps even by oneself. 'Yes, of course!' one would think. 'That's it. I've known that for some time. It's just that I haven't actually heard it put like that, I hadn't grasped it . . .'

(From *Memoirs of a Survivor* (The Octagon Press, London, 1974))

EXERCISE 2

Would you say that this passage from Joe Orton's *Loot* was effective in its subversion of conventional values? Or is it simply anarchic and immoral? Is the text 'carnivalised'? Does it resist 'containment'? Does 'style' play a part in giving the subversiveness a sharper edge (see sections 13 and 24)?

Explore the horizon of expectations which is implied by the play and which would have been shared by an audience. Does this affect the interpretation an audience would have made of the passage? Consider how a changed horizon (ours for example) would alter the text's significance (see section 18).

Truscott.	We've had the tabs on her for years. Thirteen fatal accidents, two cases of suspected fish poisoning. One unexplained disappearance. She's practised her own form of genocide for a decade and called it nursing.
Fay	(*staring at him, agitatedly*). I never killed anyone.
Truscott.	At the George V hospital in Holyhead eighty-seven people died within a week. How do you explain that?
Fay.	It was the geriatric ward. They were old.
Truscott.	They had a right to live, same as anybody else.
Fay.	I was in the children's ward.
Truscott.	How many innocents did you massacre – Phyllis?
Fay.	None.
Truscott.	I fail to see why you choose to cloak the episode in mystery. You can't escape.
Fay.	Mrs McLeavy accused her husband.
Truscott.	We can't accept the evidence of a ghost. The problems posed would be insuperable.
Fay.	You must prove me guilty. That is the law.
Truscott.	You know nothing of the law. I know nothing of the law. That makes us equal in the sight of the law.
Fay.	I'm innocent till I'm proved guilty. This is a free country. The law is impartial.
Truscott.	Who's been filling your head with that rubbish?
Fay.	I can't be had for anything. You've no proof.
Truscott.	When I make out my report I shall say that you've given me a confession. It could prejudice your case if I have to forge one.
Fay.	I shall deny that I've confessed.
Truscott.	Perjury is a serious crime.
Fay.	Have you no respect for the truth?
Truscott.	We have a saying under the blue lamp 'Waste time on the truth and you'll be pounding the beat until the day you retire.'
Fay	(*breaking down*). The British police force used to be run by men of integrity.

Truscott. That is a mistake which has been rectified. Come along now. I
can't stand here all day.

Fay   (*drying her eyes*). My name is Phyllis Jean McMahon alias Fay
Jean McMahon. I am twenty-eight years of age and a nurse by
profession. On the third of December last I advertised in the
trade papers for a situation. Mr McLeavy answered my request.
He wished me to nurse his wife back to health: a task I found
impossible to perform. Mrs McLeavy was dying. Had eutha-
nasia not been against my religion I would have practised it.
Instead I decided to murder her. I administered poison during
the night of June the twenty-second. In the morning I found
her dead and notified the authorities. I have had nothing but
heartache ever since. I am sorry for my dreadful crime. (*She
weeps.*)

Truscott (*looking up from his notebook*). Very good. Your style is simple
and direct. It's a theme which less skilfully handled could've
given offence. (*He puts away his notebook.*) One of the most
accomplished confessions I've heard in some time.

(From *Loot, The Complete Plays* (Methuen, London, (1976, pp. 254–5))

EXERCISE 3

There is only one sentence of comment by the narrator in the first extract from Jane Austen's *Emma*. How important is it? How do you establish your critical bearings when you read it? Without this sentence the passage might be a dialogue in a play. Would it be possible to establish an 'implied author' in the dialogue (see section 3)? Assuming that Jane Austen exposes Emma's superior attitude to the lower classes in both passages, what sort of social values are implied as positives? It will be necessary to read a larger portion of the novel in order to discern the form of its representation of social relations, or of its reworking of contemporary ideological discourses (see sections 22 and 24).

The subtlety of Jane Austen's irony has often been noted. Such irony requires a very precise and unambiguous use of language, because irony depends on a fixed, though unstated, value system. Modern literary theory usually questions the possibility of stable signification. Do you see any ways in which readers might produce more than one meaning from the passage (see sections 10 and 15)?

(a)
'Miss Woodhouse, as you will not give me your opinion, I must do as well as I can by myself; and I have now quite determined, and really almost made up my mind – to refuse Mr Martin. Do you think I am right?'

'Perfectly, perfectly right, my dearest Harriet; you are doing just what you ought. While you were at all in suspense I kept my feelings to myself, but now that you are so completely decided I have no hesitation in approving. Dear Harriet, I give myself joy of this. It would have grieved me to lose your acquaintance, which must have been the consequence of your marrying Mr Martin. While you were in the smallest degree wavering, I said nothing about it, because I would not influence; but it would have been the loss of a friend to me. I could not have visited Mrs Robert Martin, of Abbey-Mill Farm. Now I am secure of you for ever.'

Harriet had not surmised her own danger, but the idea of it struck her forcibly.

'You could not have visited me!' she cried, looking aghast. 'No, to be sure you could not; but I never thought of that before. That would have been too dreadful! – What an escape! – Dear Miss Woodhouse, I would not give up the pleasure and honour of being intimate with you for anything in the world.'

'Indeed, Harriet, it would have been a severe pang to lose you; but it must have been. You would have thrown yourself out of all good society. I must have given you up.'

'Dear me! – How should I ever have borne it! It would have killed me never to come to Hartfield any more!'

'Dear affectionate creature! – *You* banished to Abbey-Mill Farm! – *You* confined to the society of the illiterate and vulgar all your life! I wonder how the young man could have the assurance to ask it. He must have a pretty good opinion of himself.'

'I do not think he is conceited either, in general,' said Harriet, her conscience opposing such censure; 'at least he is very good natured, and I shall always feel much obliged to him, and have a great regard for – but that is quite a different thing from – and you know, though he may like me, it does not follow that I should – and certainly I must confess that since my visiting here I have seen people – and if one comes to compare them, person and manners, there is no comparison at all, *one* is so very handsome and agreeable. However, I do really think Mr Martin a very amiable young man, and have a great opinion of him; and his being so much attached to me – and his writing such a letter – but as to leaving you, it is what I would not do upon any consideration.'

'Thank you, thank you, my own sweet little friend. We will not be parted. A woman is not to marry a man merely because she is asked, or because he is attached to her, and can write a tolerable letter.'

(b)

They were now approaching the cottage, and all idle topics were superseded. Emma was very compassionate; and the distresses of the poor were as sure of relief from her personal attention and kindness, her counsel and her patience, as from her purse. She understood their ways, could allow for their ignorance and their temptations, had no romantic expectations of extraordinary virtue from those, for whom education had done so little; entered into their troubles with ready sympathy, and always gave her assistance with as much intelligence as good-will. In the present instance, it was sickness and poverty together which she came to visit; and after remaining there as long as she could give comfort or advice, she quitted the cottage with such an impression of the scene as made her say to Harriet, as they walked away,

'These are the sights, Harriet, to do one good. How trifling they make every thing else appear! – I feel now as if I could think of nothing but these poor creatures all the rest of the day; and yet, who can say how soon it may all vanish from my mind?'

'Very true,' said Harriet. 'Poor creatures! one can think of nothing else.'

'And really, I do not think the impression will soon be over,' said Emma, as she crossed the low hedge, and tottering footstep which ended the narrow, slippery path through the cottage garden, and brought them into the lane again. 'I do not think it will,' stopping to look once more at all the outward wretchedness of the place, and recall the still greater within.

'Oh! dear, no,' said her companion.

They walked on. The lane made a slight bend; and when that bend was passed, Mr Elton was immediately in sight; and so near as to give Emma time only to say farther,

'Ah! Harriet, here comes a very sudden trial of our stability in good thoughts. Well, (smiling,) I hope it may be allowed that if compassion has produced exertion and relief to the sufferers, it has done all that is truly important. If we feel for the wretched, enough to do all we can for them, the rest is empty sympathy, only distressing to ourselves.'

(From *Emma* (Penguin, Harmondsworth, 1966, pp. 80–1, 111)

EXERCISE 4

Attempt a 'deconstruction' of this passage from John Berger's *A Fortunate Man* about Sassall the country doctor. The central binary opposition seems to be 'common sense' and 'philosophy'. Berger's attack on common sense requires that 'philosophy' become the privileged term. How would you go about reversing the hierarchy? Could one argue that the passage deconstructs itself (see sections 7, 12 and 14)? On a different tack, try discussing the passage as an account of 'ideology' (see section 22).

> In general his patients think of Sassall as 'belonging' to their community. He represents no outside interest – in such an area any outside interest suggests exploitation. He is trusted. Yet this is not the same thing as saying that he is thought of or treated as an equal. [. . .]
> He is privileged because of the way he can think and can talk! If the estimate of his privilege was strictly logical, it would include the fact of his education and his medical training. But that was a long time ago, whereas the evidence of the way he thinks – not purely medically but in general – is there every time he is there. It is why the villagers talk to him, why they tell him the local news, why they listen, why they wonder whether his unusual views are right, why some say 'He's a wonderful doctor but not what you'd expect', and why some middle-class neigbours call him a crack-pot.
> The villagers do not consider him privileged because they find his thinking so impressive. It is the style of his thinking which they immediately recognize as different from theirs. They depend upon common-sense and he does not.
> It is generally thought that common-sense is practical. It is practical only in a short-term view. Common-sense declares that it is foolish to bite the hand that feeds you. But it is foolish only up to the moment when you realize that you might be fed very much better. In the long-term view common-sense is passive because it is based on the acceptance of an outdated view of the possible. The body of common-sense has to accrue too slowly. All its propositions have to be proved so many times before they can become unquestionable, i.e. traditional. When they become traditional they gain oracular authority. Hence the strong element of *superstition* always evident in 'practical' common-sense.
> Common-sense is part of the home-made ideology of those who have been deprived of fundamental learning, of those who have been kept ignorant. This ideology is compounded from different sources: items that have survived from religion, items of empirical knowledge, items of protective scepticism, items culled for comfort from the superficial learning that *is* supplied. But the point is that common-sense can never teach itself, can never advance beyond its own limits, for as soon as the lack of fundamental learning has been made good, all items become questionable and the whole function of common-sense is destroyed.

Common-sense can only exist as a category insofar as it can be distinguished from the spirit of enquiry, from philosophy.

Common-sense is essentially *static*. It belongs to the ideology of those who are socially passive, never understanding what or who has made their situation as it is. But it represents only a part – and often a small part – of their character. These same people say or do many things which are an affront to their own common-sense. And when they justify something by saying 'It's only common-sense', this is frequently an apology for denying or betraying some of their deepest feelings or instincts.

Sassall accepts his innermost feelings and intuitions as clues. His own self is often his most promising starting-point. His aim is to find what may be hidden in others:

'I don't find it hard to express uncensored thoughts or sentiments but when I do, it keeps on occurring to me that this is a form of self-indulgence. That sounds somewhat pompous, but still. At least it makes me realize and understand why patients thank me so profusely for merely listening: they too are apologizing for what they think – wrongly – is their self-indulgence.'

Using his own mortality as another starting-point he needs to find references of hope or possibility in an almost unimaginable future.

'I'm encouraged by the fact that the molecules of this table and glass and plant are rearranged to make you or me, and that the bad things are perhaps badly arranged molecules and therefore capable maybe of reorganization one day.'

Yet however fanciful his speculations, he returns to measure them by the standards of actual knowledge to date. And then from this measurement begins to speculate again.

'You never know *for certain* about anything. This sounds falsely modest and trite, but it's the honest truth. Most of the time you are right and you do *appear* to know, but every now and then the rules seem to get broken and then you realize how lucky you have been on the occasions when *you think you have known* and have been proved correct.'

He never stops speculating, testing, comparing. The more open the question the more it interests him.

Such a way of thinking demands the right to be theoretical and to be concerned with generalizations. Yet theory and generalizations belong by their nature to the cities or the distant capital where the big general decisions are always made. Furthermore, to arrive at general decisions and theories one needs to travel in order to gain experience. Nobody travels from the Forest. So nobody in the Forest has either the power or the means to theorize. They are 'practical' people.

(From *A Fortunate Man: The Story of a Country Doctor* (Penguin, Harmondsworth, 1969, pp. 101–3))

EXERCISE 5

This poem by John Donne describes the demise of the 'subject' ('I'): the speaker has been deprived of a recognisable 'subject position' by the lady's death. Does the poem cast doubt upon the substantial nature of personal identity? Some have argued that all Donne's poems project a strong sense of personal identity. Can both views be correct (see sections 10 and 11)?

In what ways does the poem work upon (rework) Christian ideology (especially the fundamental dichotomies of soul/body, heaven/earth, life/afterlife) and in so doing does the poem reveal the inner contradictions of that ideology (see section 22)?

A Nocturnal upon S. Lucy's Day,
being the shortest day

'Tis the year's midnight, and it is the day's,
Lucy's, who scarce seven hours herself unmasks,
    The sun is spent, and now his flasks
    Send forth light squibs, no constant rays;
      The world's whole sap is sunk:
The general balm th' hydroptic earth hath drunk,
Whither, as to the bed's-feet, life is shrunk,
Dead and interred; yet all these seem to laugh,
Compared with me, who am their epitaph.

Study me then, you who shall lovers be
At the next world, that is, at the next spring:
    For I am every dead thing,
    In whom love wrought new alchemy.
      For his art did express
A quintessence even from nothingness,
From dull privations, and lean emptiness
He ruined me, and I am re-begot
Of absence, darkness, death; things which are not.

All others, from all things, draw all that's good,
Life, soul, form, spirit, whence they being have;
    I, by love's limbeck, am the grave
    Of all, that's nothing. Oft a flood
      Have we two wept, and so
Drowned the whole world, us two; oft did we grow
To be two chaoses, when we did show
Care to aught else; and often absences
Withdrew our souls, and made us carcases.

But I am by her death (which word wrongs her)
Of the first nothing, the elixir grown;

Were I a man, that I were one,
I needs must know; I should prefer,
    If I were any beast,
Some ends, some means; yea plants, yea stones detest,
And love; all, all some properties invest;
If I an ordinary nothing were,
As shadow, a light, and body must be here.

But I am none; nor will my sun renew.
You lovers, for whose sake, the lesser sun
    At this time to the Goat is run
    To fetch new lust, and give it you,
        Enjoy your summer all;
Since she enjoys her long night's festival,
Let me prepare towards her, and let me call
This hour her vigil, and her eve, since this
Both the year's, and the day's deep midnight is.
(From The Complete English Poems, ed. A. J. Smith (Penguin, Harmonds-
worth, 1971, pp. 72–3))

EXERCISE 6

Does this sonnet by Edna St Vincent Millay bear the marks of being written by a woman? Could a man have written it as a 'dramatic monologue', for example? Does our sense of the poet's gender make any difference to our interpretation? Do you imagine that a female reader would interpret the poem differently from a male reader (see sections 20 and 21)?

SONNET XLI

I, being born a woman and distressed
By all the needs and notions of my kind,
Am urged by your propinquity to find
Your person fair, and feel a certain zest
To bear your body's weight upon my breast:
So subtly is the fume of life designed,
To clarify the pulse and cloud the mind,
And leave me once again undone, possessed.
Think not for this, however, the poor treason
Of my stout blood against my staggering brain,
I shall remember you with love, or season
My scorn with pity, – let me make it plain:
I find this frenzy insufficient reason
For conversation when we meet again.
(From *Norton Anthology of Poetry*, 3rd edn (W. W. Norton, New York and London, 1983, pp. 1033–4))

EXERCISE 7

The text of this short poem, 'Infant Sorrow', is divorced from William Blake's illuminated plate. In this form the text is highly enigmatic ('open'). Consider a range of approaches to interpretation: psychological, feminist, New Historical, Marxist, and reader-response (see the appropriate sections).

My mother groand! my father wept.
Into the dangerous world I leapt:
Helpless, naked, piping loud;
Like a fiend hid in a cloud.

Struggling in my father's hands,
Striving against my swadling bands,
Bound and weary I thought best
To sulk upon my mother's breast.
(From *Poetry and Prose*, ed. Geoffrey Keynes (Nonesuch Press, London, 1961, p. 76))

EXERCISE 8

Cleanth Brooks and Robert Penn Warren, in their influential *Understanding Poetry* (1938), argued that this poem by Andrew Marvell 'The Definition of Love' expressed through its poetic imagery a 'complex and rich experience'. The paradoxes of the opening stanzas, they suggest, help us to grasp the poet's 'complex' attitude. Can you see any limitations in their approach? Think about the terms 'complex' and 'experience'. What do they imply about reading and writing? Compare the Brooks and Warren approach with a 'deconstructive' reading of the poem. Think about the different assumptions about ideas, language and ideology underlying the two approaches (see Introduction and sections 2, 12 and 14).

Try using a Russian Formalist or structuralist approach to the poem, employing the concepts of defamiliarisation or binary opposition (metaphor and metonymy, for example) (see sections 5, 7 and 9).

My Love is of a birth as rare
As 'tis for object strange and high:
It was begotten by despair
Upon Impossibility.

Magnanimous Despair alone
Could show me so divine a thing,
Where feeble Hope could ne'r have flown
But vainly flapped its Tinsel Wing.

And yet I quickly might arrive
Where my extended Soul is fixed,
But Fate does iron wedges drive,
And always crowds itself betwixt.

For Fate with jealous Eye does see
Two perfect Loves, nor lets them close:
Their union would her ruin be,
And her Tyrannic power depose.

And therefore her Decrees of Steel
Us as the distant Poles have plac'd,
(Though Love's whole World on us doth wheel)
Not by themselves to be embrac'd,

Unless the giddy Heaven fall,
And Earth some new Convulsion tear,
And, us to join, the World should all
Be cramped into a Planisphere.

As Lines, so Loves oblique may well
Themselves in every Angle greet;
But ours, so truly Parallel,
Though infinite, can never meet.

Therefore the love which us doth bind,
But Fate so enviously debars,
Is the Conjuction of the Mind,
And Opposition of the Stars.
(From *Poems and Letters*, ed. H. M. Margoliouth, 2 vols, 3rd edn
(Clarendon Press, Oxford, New York, 1971, I. 140–1))

EXERCISE 9

Noam Chomsky, writing about the Vietnam war, coined the term 'insane rationality' to describe American militarism. Examine the effects of Joseph Heller's comic style on your perception of American militarism as represented in this extract from *Catch 22*. Does he reveal something about militarism which only fiction could reveal (see sections 22 and 24)? Does the passage reflect an 'alienated' society (see section 23)?

Think about the defamiliarisation of religion in the passage (see section 5).

Is the reference to young girls' breasts sexist? Is your answer affected by your own sexual identity? Is the whole passage obviously written by a man (see sections 20 and 21)?

> After a while he realized that he was staring at rows and rows of bushels of red plum tomatoes and grew so intrigued by the question of what bushels brimming with red plum tomatoes were doing in a group commander's office that he forgot completely about the discussion of prayer meetings until Colonel Cathcart, in a genial digression, inquired:
> "Would you like to buy some, Chaplain? They come right off the farm Colonel Korn and I have up in the hills. I can let you have a bushel wholesale."
> "Oh, no, sir. I don't think so."
> "That's quite all right," the colonel assured him liberally. "You don't have to. Milo is glad to snap up all we can produce. These were picked only yesterday. Notice how firm and ripe they are, like a young girl's breasts."
> The chaplain blushed, and the colonel understood at once that he had made a mistake. He lowered his head in shame, his cumbersome face burning. His fingers felt gross and unwieldy. He hated the chaplain venomously for being a chaplain and making a coarse blunder out of an observation that in any other circumstances, he knew, would have been considered witty and urbane. He tried miserably to recall some means of extricating them both from their devastating embarrassment. He recalled instead that the chaplain was only a captain, and he straightened at once with a shocked and outraged gasp. His cheeks grew tight with fury at the thought that he had just been duped into humiliation by a man who was almost the same age as he was and still only a captain, and he swung upon the chaplain avengingly with a look of such murderous antagonism that the chaplain began to tremble. The colonel punished him sadistically with a long, glowering, malignant, hateful, silent stare.
> "We were speaking about something else," he reminded the chaplain cuttingly at last. "We were not speaking about the firm, ripe breasts of beautiful young girls but about something else entirely. We were speaking

about conducting religious services in the briefing room before each mission. Is there any reason why we can't?"

"No, sir," the chaplain mumbled.

"Then we'll begin with this afternoon's mission." The colonel's hostility softened gradually as he applied himself to details. "Now, I want you to give a lot of thought to the kind of prayers we're going to say. I don't want anything heavy or sad. I'd like you to keep it light and snappy, something that will send the boys out feeling pretty good. Do you know what I mean? I don't want any of this Kingdom of God or Valley of Death stuff. That's all too negative. What are you making such a sour face for?"

"I'm sorry, sir," the chaplain stammered. "I happened to be thinking of the Twenty-third Psalm just as you said that."

"How does that one go?"

"That's the one you were just referring to, sir. 'The Lord is my shepherd; I –'"

"That's the one I was just referring to. It's out. What else have you got?"

"'Save me, O God; for the waters are come in unto –'"

"No waters," the colonel decided, blowing ruggedly into his cigarette holder after flipping the butt down into his combed-brass ash tray. "Why don't we try something musical? How about the harps on the willows?"

"That has the rivers of Babylon in it, sir," the chaplain replied. "'. . . there we sat down, yea, we wept, when we remembered Zion.'"

"Zion? Let's forget about *that* one right now. I'd like to know how that one even got in there. Haven't you got anything humorous that stays away from waters and valleys and God? I'd like to keep away from the subject of religion altogether if we can."

The chaplain was apologetic. "I'm sorry, sir, but just about all the prayers I know are rather somber in tone and make at least some passing reference to God."

"Then let's get some new ones. The men are already doing enough bitching about the missions I send them on without our rubbing it in with any sermons about God or death or Paradise. Why can't we take a more positive approach? Why can't we all pray for something good, like a tighter bomb pattern, for example? Couldn't we pray for a tighter bomb pattern?"

(From *Catch 22* (Jonathan Cape, London, 1955, pp. 206–7))

EXERCISE 10

Consider how Fielding, in this passage from *Joseph Andrews*, uses devices to defamiliarise the social distinctions based upon 'fashion'. Compare this approach with a Marxist or structuralist interpretation of the passage (see sections 5, 6–9, 19, 22–4).

Be it known then, that the human Species are divided into two sorts of People, to-wit, *High* People and *Low* People. As by High People, I would not be understood to mean Persons literally born higher in their Dimensions than the rest of the Species, nor metaphorically those of exalted Characters or Abilites; so by Low People I cannot be construed to intend the Reverse. High People signify no other than People of Fashion, and low People those of no Fashion. Now this word *Fashion*, hath by long use lost its original Meaning, from which at present it gives us a very different Idea: for I am deceived, if by Persons of Fashion, we do not generally include a Conception of Birth and Accomplishments superior to the Herd of Mankind; whereas in reality, nothing more was originally meant by a Person of Fashion, than a Person who drest himself in the Fashion of the Times; and the Word really and truly signifies no more at this day. Now the World being thus divided into People of Fashion, and People of no Fashion, a fierce Contention arose between them, nor would those of one Party, to avoid Suspicion, be seen publickly to speak to those of the other; tho' they often held a very good Correspondence in private. In this Contention, it is difficult to say which Party succeeded: for whilst the People of Fashion seized several Places to their own use, such as Courts, Assemblies, Operas, Balls, &c. the People of no Fashion, besides one Royal Place called his Majesty's Bear-Garden, have been in constant Possession of all Hops, Fairs, Revels, &c. Two Places have been agreed to be divided between them, namely the Church and the Play-House; where they segregate themselves from each other in a remarkable Manner: for as the People of Fashion exalt themselves at Church over the Heads of the People of no Fashion; so in the Play-House they abase themselves in the same degree under their Feet. This Distinction I have never met with any one able to account for; it is sufficient, that so far from looking on each other as Brethren in the Christian Language, they seem scarce to regard each other as of the same Species. This the Terms *strange Persons, People one does not know, the Creature, Wretches, Beasts, Brutes*, and many other Appellations evidently demonstrate; [. . . .] these two Parties, especially those bordering nearly on each other, to-wit the lowest of the High, and the highest of the Low, often change their Parties according to Place and Time; for those who are People of Fashion in one place, are often People of no Fashion in another: And with regard to Time, it may not be unpleasant to survey the Picture of Dependance like a kind of Ladder; (Book II, chapter 13)

(From *Joseph Andrews and Shamela*, ed. Douglas Brooks (Oxford University Press, London, Oxford and New York, 1971, pp. 140–1))

EXERCISE 11

In the first passage from Shakespeare's *As You Like It* Orlando is in
danger of his life from the malice of his elder brother Oliver. Adam, an
old family retainer, warns him of the danger and offers to sacrifice his
hard-earned savings to help Orlando to escape. In the second passage,
Rosalind and Celia, in the forest of Arden, ask the shepherd Corin for
food and shelter. His master is about to make him redundant, but the
ladies are able to solve the problem with cash.

Discuss the passages from a Marxist viewpoint, taking into account
the representation of economic relations (see section 24).

(a) *Rosalind.* I prithee shepherd, if that love or gold
             Can in this desert place buy entertainment,
             Bring us where we may rest ourselves and feed.
             Here's a young maid with travel much oppress'd,
             And faints for succour.
    Corin.   Fair sir, I pity her,
             And wish, for her sake more than for mine own,
             My fortunes were more able to relieve her;
             But I am shepherd to another man,
             And do not shear the fleeces that I graze.
             My master is of churlish disposition,
             And little recks to find the way to heaven
             By doing deeds of hospitality.
             Besides, his cote, his flocks, and bounds of feed
             Are now on sale, and at our sheepcote now
             By reason of his absence there is nothing
             That you will feed on. But what is, come see,
             And in my voice most welcome shall you be.
    Rosalind. What is he that shall buy his flock and pasture?
    Corin. That young swain that you saw here but erewhile,
             That little cares for buying anything.
    Rosalind. I pray thee, if it stand with honesty,
             Buy thou the cottage, pasture, and the flock,
             And thou shalt have to pay for it of us.
    Celia. And we will mend thy wages. I like this place,
             And willingly could waste my time in it.

(b) *Adam.* I have five hundred crowns,
             The thrifty hire I sav'd under your father,
             Which I did store to be my foster-nurse,
             When service should in my old limbs lie lame,
             And unregarded age in corners thrown.
             Take that, and He that doth the ravens feed,

Yea providently caters for the sparrow,
Be comfort to my age. Here is the gold,
All this I give you. Let me be your servant.
Though I look old, yet I am strong and lusty;
For in my youth I never did apply
Hot and rebellious liquors in my blood,
Nor did not with unbashful forehead woo
The means of weakness and debility.
Therefore my age is as a lusty winter,
Frosty, but kindly. Let me go with you,
I'll do the service of a younger man
In all your business and necessities.

Orlando. O good old man, how well in thee appears
The constant service of the antique world,
When service sweat for duty, not for meed.
Thou art not for the fashion of these times,
Where none will sweat but for promotion,
And having that, do choke their service up
Even with the having; it is not so with thee.

EXERCISE 12

Do you think that female readers would find the treatment of Mrs Whiston in this opening passage from D. H. Lawrence's story 'The White Stocking' more irritating than male readers? Is the passage obviously written by a man or not? Answer this with close reference to details in the text (see sections 20 and 21).

Register the precise stages through which you pass in building up a 'gestalt' image of the two characters as you read. What adjustments did you make as you proceeded, and what textual features triggered the adjustments? What questions remain in your mind as unsolved at each point? Can you identify any 'gaps' in the passage which you are forced to fill provisionally? What options for filling them occur to you (see section 17)?

Use Barthes' codes as a method of reading the passage. Divide the text into 'lexias' following Barthes' method in S/Z (see section 16).

What sort of narration occurs in this passage? Is there a 'focaliser'? Read the entire story and then apply Greimas' actantial scheme to it (see section 8).

Can you detect any interplay of 'binary oppositions' in the text (see section 7)?

'I'm getting up, Teddilinks,' said Mrs. Whiston, and she sprang out of bed briskly.

'What the Hanover's got you?' asked Whiston.

'Nothing. Can't I get up?' she replied animatedly.

It was about seven o'clock, scarcely light yet in the cold bedroom. Whiston lay still and looked at his wife. She was a pretty little thing, with her fleecy, short black hair all tousled. He watched her as she dressed quickly, flicking her small, delightful limbs, throwing her clothes about her. Her slovenliness and untidiness did not trouble him. When she picked up the edge of her petticoat, ripped off a torn string of white lace, and flung it on the dressing-table, her careless abandon made his spirit glow. She stood before the mirror and roughly scrambled together her profuse little mane of hair. He watched the quickness and softness of her young shoulders, calmly, like a husband, and appreciatively.

'Rise up,' she cried, turning to him with a quick wave of her arm – 'and shine forth.'

They had been married two years. But still, when she had gone out of the room, he felt as if all his light and warmth were taken away, he became aware of the raw, cold morning. So he rose himself, wondering casually what had roused her so early. Usually she lay in bed as late as she could.

Whiston fastened a belt round his loins and went downstairs in shirt and trousers. He heard her singing in her snatchy fashion. The stairs creaked under his weight. He passed down the narrow little passage, which she called a hall, of the seven and sixpenny house which was his first home.

He was a shapely young fellow of about twenty-eight, sleepy now and easy with well-being. He heard the water drumming into the kettle, and she began to whistle. He loved the quick way she dodged the supper cups under the tap to wash them for breakfast. She looked an untidy minx, but she was quick and handy enough.

'Teddilinks,' she cried.

'What?'

'Light a fire, quick.'

She wore an old, sack-like dressing-jacket of black silk pinned across her breast. But one of the sleeves, coming unfastened, showed some delightful pink upper-arm.

'Why don't you sew your sleeve up?' he said, suffering from the sight of the exposed soft flesh.

'Where?' she cried, peering round. 'Nuisance,' she said, seeing the gap, then with light fingers went on drying the cups.

The kitchen was of fair size, but gloomy. Whiston poked out the dead ashes.

Suddenly a thud was heard at the door down the passage.

'I'll go,' cried Mrs. Whiston, and she was gone down the hall. [. . .]

She tore open the thin envelope. There was a long, hideous, cartoon valentine. She smiled briefly and dropped it on the floor. [. . .] The third envelope contained another white packet – apparently a cotton handkerchief neatly folded. She shook it out. It was a long white stocking, but there was a little weight in the toe. Quickly, she thrust down her arm, wriggling her fingers into the toe of the stocking, and brought out a small box. She peeped inside the box, then hastily opened a door on her left hand, and went into the little cold sitting-room. She had her lower lip caught earnestly between her teeth.

With a little flash of triumph, she lifted a pair of pearl ear-rings from the small box, and she went to the mirror. There, earnestly, she began to hook them through her ears, looking at herself sideways in the glass. Curiously concentrated and intent she seemed as she fingered the lobes of her ears, her head bent on one side.

(From 'The White Stocking' in *The Collected Short Stories*, vol. I (Penguin, New York, 1933, pp. 230–1))

EXERCISE 13

The narrator of this passage from Norman Mailer's *An American Dream* is Rojack, the central character of the novel who murders his wife Deborah. What sort of narrator is he? What values are implied in the narration (see sections 3 and 8)? Does the passage express an essentially 'masculine' attitude? What features of the passage – narrative form, imagery, or characterisation – could be regarded as 'masculine' or even misogynist? Is Mailer right to claim that the attitudes of his characters should not be attributed to him personally? If he were right, would this satisfy feminist objections (see section 20)? What light does psychoanalysis throw upon the passage (see section 11)?

> I hated her more than not by now, my life with her had been a series of successes cancelled by quick failures, and I knew so far as I could still keep any confidence that she had done her best to birth each loss, she was an artist at sucking the marrow from a broken bone, she worked each side of the street with a skill shared only in common by the best of street-walkers and the most professional of heiresses. Once, for an instance, at a party, a friend of hers, a man I was never able to like, a man who never liked me, had proceeded to beat on me so well for "celebrity" on television that he was carried away. He invited me to box. Well, we were both drunk. But when it came to boxing I was a good *torero de salon*. I was not bad with four drinks and furniture to circle about. So we sparred to the grim amusement and wild consternation of the ladies, the sober evaluation of the gents. I was feeling mean. I roughed him up a hitch or two in the clinches, I slapped at him at will with my jab, holding my hand open but swinging the slaps in, he was such an ass, and after it went on for a minute, he was beginning in compensation to throw his punches as hard (and wild) as he could, whereas I was deepening into concentration. Which is the first reward of the ring. I was sliding my moves off the look in his eye and the shift of his fists, I had settled into the calm of a pregnant typhoon, the kill was sweet and up in me, I could feel it twenty moves away, he was going to finish with three slugs to the belly and his arms apart, that is what it would take, his eye was sweaty and I was going keen. Just then his wife broke in. "Stop!" she cried, "absolutely stop!" and came between us.
>
> He was a bad type. "Why'd you stop it?" he asked. "It was going to be fun."
>
> "Fun!" she said, "you were going to get killed."
>
> Well, the point to the story is that when I turned around to wink at Deborah – she had heard me talk much about boxing but had never seen me fight – I discovered she had quit the room.
>
> "Of course I left," she said later, "it was a sight, bullying that poor man."

"Poor? He's bigger than I am."

"And ten years older."

That took the taste away. Next time some passing friend invited me to spar at a party – not until a year later I believe, not *all* the parties ended in a bout – I refused. He filed the needle to a point. I still refused. When we got home, she told me I was afraid.

It was worth little to refer to the first episode. "This man, at least," she said, "was younger than you."

"I could have taken him."

"I don't believe it. Your mouth was weak, and you were perspiring."

When I looked into myself I was not certain any longer that there had been no fear. So it took on prominence for me. I did not know any longer.

One could multiply that little puncture by a thousand; Deborah was an artist with the needle, and never pinked you twice on the same spot. (Unless it had turned to ulcer.) So I hated her, yes indeed I did, but my hatred was a cage which wired my love, and I did not know if I had the force to find my way free. Marriage to her was the armature of my ego; remove the armature and I might topple like clay. When I was altogether depressed by myself it seemed as if she were the only achievement to which I could point – I finally had been the man whom Deborah Caughlin Mangaravidi Kelly had lived with in marriage, and since she'd been notorious in her day, picking and choosing among a gallery of beaux: politicians of the first rank, racing drivers, tycoons, and her fair share of the more certified playboys of the Western world, she had been my entry to the big league. I had loved her with the fury of my ego, that way I loved her still, but I loved her the way a drum majorette loved the power of the band for the swell it gave to each little strut. If I was a war hero, an ex-Congressman, a professor of popular but somewhat notorious reputation, and a star of sorts on a television show which I cannot here even bear to explain, if I also had a major work on existential psychology, a herculean endeavour of six to twenty volumes which would (ideally) turn Freud on his head (but remained still in my own head) I had also the secret ambition to return to politics. I had the idea of running some day for Senator, an operation which would not be possible without the vast connections of Deborah's clan.

(From *An American Dream* (André Deutsch, London, (1965), pp. 22–4))

EXERCISE 14

In what ways does this passage from the beginning of John Barth's *Chimera* involve 'baring the device'? Think especially about the story's reflections on story telling. What is the effect of presenting Scheherazade's sister's story in quotation marks without an external narrator's intervention (see sections 4 and 8)? How might the reader respond to this opening? What deductions, provisional assumptions and uncertainties arise in your mind as you read? Does the author intend to tease the reader, do you think (see sections 15–18)?

"At this point I interrupted my sister as usual to say, 'You have a way with words, Scheherazade. This is the thousandth night I've sat at the foot of your bed while you and the King made love and you told him stories, and the one in progress holds me like a genie's gaze. I wouldn't dream of breaking in like this, just before the end, except that I hear the first rooster crowing in the east, et cetera, and the King really ought to sleep a bit before daybreak. I wish I had your talent.'

"And as usual Sherry replied, 'You're the ideal audience, Dunyazade. But this is nothing; wait till you hear the ending, tomorrow night! Always assuming this auspicious King doesn't kill me before breakfast, as he's been going to do these thirty-three and a third months.'

"'Hmp,' said Shahryar. 'Don't take your critics for granted; I may get around to it yet. But I agree with your little sister that this is a good one you've got going, with its impostures that become authentic, its ups and downs and flights to other worlds. I don't know how in the world you dream them up.'

"'Artists have their tricks,' Sherry replied. We three said good night then, six goodnights in all. In the morning your brother went off to court, enchanted by Sherry's story. Daddy came to the palace for the thousandth time with a shroud under his arm, expecting to be told to cut his daughter's head off [. . .] Sherry and I, after the first fifty nights or so, were simply relieved when Shahryar would hmp and say, 'By Allah, I won't kill her till I've heard the end of her story'; but it still took Daddy by surprise every morning. He groveled gratitude per usual; the King per usual spent the day in his durbar, bidding and forbidding between man and man, as the saying goes; I climbed in with Sherry as soon as he was gone, and per usual we spent *our* day sleeping in and making love.

(From *Chimera* (André Deutsch, London, 1974, pp. 1–2))

EXERCISE 15

This is the opening of Tennessee Williams' *Glass Menagerie*. Roman Jakobson believed that film is oriented to metonymy and drama to metaphor. Does this passage confirm his claim? Do Tom's words suggest that drama is metaphoric (see section 9)?

What effect does the 'baring of the device' (self-conscious reference to the play) have on the reader or audience (see section 4)?

What sort of play do Tom's introductory remarks lead you to expect (see section 17)?

> *The narrator is an undisguised convention of the play. He takes whatever license with dramatic convention is convenient to his purposes.*
>
> *Tom enters, dressed as a merchant sailor, and strolls across to the fire escape. There he stops and lights a cigarette. He addresses the audience.*

Tom. Yes, I have tricks in my pocket, I have things up my sleeve. But I am the opposite of a stage magician. He gives you illusion that has the appearance of truth. I give you truth in the pleasant disguise of illusion.

To begin with, I turn back time. I reverse it to that quaint period, the thirties, when the huge middle class of America was matriculating in a school for the blind. Their eyes had failed them, or they had failed their eyes, and so they were having their fingers pressed forcibly down on the fiery Braille alphabet of a dissolving economy.

In Spain there was revolution. Here there was only shouting and confusion. In Spain there was Guernica. Here there were disturbances of labor, sometimes pretty violent, in otherwise peaceful cities such as Chicago, Cleveland, Saint Louis. . . . This is the social background of the play.

> *Music begins to play.*

The play is memory. Being a memory play, it is dimly lighted, it is sentimental, it is not realistic. In memory everything seems to happen to music. That explains the fiddle in the wings.

I am the narrator of the play, and also a character in it. The other characters are my mother, Amanda, my sister, Laura, and a gentleman caller who appears in the final scenes. He is the most realistic character in the play, being an emissary from a world of reality that we were somehow set apart from. But since I have a poet's weakness for symbols, I am using this character also as a symbol; he is the long-delayed but always expected something that we live for.

There is a fifth character in the play who doesn't appear except in this larger-than-life-size photograph over the mantel. This is our father who left us a long time ago. He was a telephone man who fell in love with long distances; he gave up his job with the telephone company and skipped the light fantastic out of town. . . .

The last we heard of him was a picture postcard from Mazatlan, on the Pacific coast of Mexico, containing a message of two words: "Hello – Goodbye!" and no address.

I think the rest of the play will explain itself. . . .

(From *The Glass Menagerie*, *The Norton Introduction to Literature* (3rd edn, W. W. Norton, New York and London, 1973, pp. 1241–2))

EXERCISE 16

Would you describe Adrienne Rich's 'Planetarium' as a feminist poem? Does her way of writing include features which you would describe as characteristic of women's writing? Consider, for example, the layout, rhythms, and imagery of the poem (see section 21).

Apply Julia Kristeva's theory of signification to the poem's psychological dimension. Does the representation of the female 'I' contain marks of the 'semiotic' drives to which Kristeva refers (see sections 10–11)?

Planetarium

(Thinking of Caroline Herschel, 1750–1848,
astronomer, sister of William; and others)

A woman in the shape of a monster
a monster in the shape of a woman
the skies are full of them

a woman   "in the snow
among the Clocks and instruments
or measuring the ground with poles"

in her 98 years to discover
8 comets

she whom the moon ruled
like us
levitating into the night sky
riding the polished lenses

Galaxies of women, there
doing penance for impetuousness
ribs chilled
in those spaces   of the mind

An eye,
          "virile, precise and absolutely certain"
          from the mad webs of Uranisborg
                              encountering the NOVA

every impulse of light exploding
from the core
as life flies out of us

          Tycho[1] whispering at last   [1] T. Brahe [astronomer]
          "Let me not seem to have lived in vain"

What we see, we see
and seeing is changing

the light that shrivels a mountain
and leaves a man alive

Heartbeat of the pulsar
heart sweating through my body

The radio impulse
pouring in from Taurus
   I am bombarded yet   I stand

I have been standing all my life in the
direct path of a battery of signals
the most accurately transmitted most
untranslatable language in the universe
I am a galactic cloud so deep so invo-
luted that a light wave could take 15
years to travel through me And has
taken I am an instrument in the shape
of a woman trying to translate pulsations
into images for the relief of the body
and the reconstruction of the mind.

    (From *The Norton Introduction to Literature* (3rd edn, W. W.
    Norton, New York and London, 1973, pp. 765–6))

EXERCISE 17

Consider the following two short passages from Virginia Woolf's *To the Lighthouse*. In the first, Lily Briscoe catches sight of Mr and Mrs Ramsay and briefly glimpses their symbolic meaning as a couple. In the second Mr Ramsay moves rapidly from rational contemplation to existential isolation. What features of the passage are characteristic of modernism and do they have distinctive ideological implications? Is Virginia Woolf undermining realism, or defining a new realism (see section 23)?

So that is marriage, Lily thought, a man and a woman looking at a girl throwing a ball. That is what Mrs. Ramsay tried to tell me the other night, she thought. For she was wearing a green shawl, and they were standing close together watching Prue and Jasper throwing catches. And suddenly the meaning which, for no reason at all, as perhaps they are stepping out of the Tube or ringing a doorbell, descends on people, making them symbolical, making them representative, came upon them, and made them in the dusk standing, looking, the symbols of marriage, husband and wife. Then, after an instant, the symbolical outline which transcended the real figures sank down again, and they became, as they met them, Mr. and Mrs. Ramsay watching the children throwing catches. (Chapter 13)

It was all familiar; this turning, that stile, that cut across the fields. Hours he would spend thus with his pipe, of an evening, thinking up and down and in and out of the old familiar lanes and commons, which were all stuck about with the history of that campaign there, the life of this statesman here, with poems and with anecdotes, with figures too, this thinker, that soldier; all very brisk and clear; but at length the lane, the field, the common, the fruitful nut-tree and the flowering hedge led him on to that further turn of the road where he dismounted always, tied his horse to a tree, and proceeded on foot alone. He reached the edge of the lawn and looked out on the bay beneath.

It was his fate, his peculiarity, whether he wished it or not, to come out thus on a spit of land which the sea is slowly eating away, and there to stand, like a desolate sea-bird, alone. It was his power, his gift, suddenly to shed all superfluities, to shrink and diminish so that he looked barer and felt sparer, even physically, yet lost none of his intensity of mind, and so to stand on his little ledge facing the dark of human ignorance, how we know nothing and the sea eats away the ground we stand on – that was his fate, his gift. (chapter 8)

(From *To the Lighthouse* (Hogarth Press, London, 1932, pp. 71–2, 114–15))

References

Althusser, Louis, *Lenin and Philosophy and Other Essays*, trans. Ben Brewster (New Left Books, London, 1971).

Arvon, Henri, *Marxist Aesthetics*, trans. H. Lane (Cornell University Press, Ithaca and London, 1973).

Bakhtin, Mikhail, *Rabelais and his World*, trans. H. Iswolsky (MIT Press, Cambridge, Mass. and London, 1968).

Bakhtin, Mikhail, *Problems of Dostoevsky's Poetics*, trans. R. W. Rotsel (Ardis, Ann Arbor, 1973).

Barber, C. L., *Shakespeare's Festive Comedy* (Princeton University Press, Princeton, NJ, 1959).

Barthes, Roland, *S/Z*, trans. Richard Miller (Jonathan Cape, London, 1975).

Benveniste, Emile, *Problems in General Linguistics* (University of Miami Press, Miami, 1971).

Bond, Edward, *Bingo: Scenes of Money and Death* (Methuen, London, 1974).

Booth, Wayne C., *The Rhetoric of Fiction* (University of Chicago Press, Chicago and London, 1961).

Bradbury, Malcolm and James McFarlane, ed., *Modernism 1890–1930* (Penguin, Harmondsworth, 1976).

Brooks, Cleanth and Robert Penn Warren, *Understanding Poetry* (3rd edn, Holt, Reinhart & Winston, New York, 1960).

Cixous, Hélène, 'The Laugh of the Medusa' in *New French Feminisms*, ed. Elaine Marks and Isabelle de Courtivron (Harvester Press, Brighton, 1981).

Culler, Jonathan, *Structuralist Poetics* (Routledge & Kegan Paul, London, 1975).

Culler, Jonathan, *The Pursuit of Signs: Semiotics, Literature, Deconstruction* (Routledge & Kegan Paul, London and Henley, 1981).

Culler, Jonathan, *On Deconstruction: Theory and Criticism after Structuralism* (Routledge & Kegan Paul, London, Melbourne and Henley, 1983).

Derrida, Jacques, *Positions*, trans. Alan Bass (Athlone Press, London, 1981).

Dollimore, Jonathan, *Radical Tragedy* (Harvester Press, Brighton, 1984).

Dollimore, Jonathan, 'Transgression and Surveillance in *Measure for Measure*' in *Political Shakespeare: New Essays in Cultural Materialism*, ed. J. Dollimore and Alan Sinfield (Manchester University Press, 1985), pp. 72–87.

Eagleton, Terry, *Marxism and Literary Criticism* (Methuen, London, 1976).

Eagleton, Terry, *Literary Theory: an Introduction* (Blackwell, Oxford, 1983).

Ellmann, Mary, *Thinking about Women* (Macmillan, London and Basingstoke, 1968; Harcourt Brace Jovanovich, New York, 1969).

Freud, Sigmund, *Art and Literature*, Pelican Freud Library, vol. 14 (Penguin, Harmondsworth, 1985).

Gadamer, Hans-Georg, *Truth and Method* (London, 1975).

Genette, Gérard, *Figures of Literary Discourse*, trans. Alan Sheridan (Blackwell, Oxford, 1982).

Greimas, A.-J., *Structural Semantics*, trans. D. McDonell (University of Nebraska Press, Lincoln and London, 1983).

Hill, Christopher, *The Century of Revolution 1603–1714* (Thomas Nelson, London, 1961).

Hill, Christopher, *Milton and the English Revolution* (Faber, London, 1977).

Holland, Norman, *5 Readers Reading* (Yale University Press, New Haven, 1975).

Holland, Norman, 'Unity Identity Self Text' in *Reader-Response Criticism from Formalism to Post-structuralism*, ed. Jane P. Tompkins (Johns Hopkins University Press, Balitmore and London, 1980), pp. 118–33.

Iser, Wolfgang, *The Act of Reading: A Theory of Aesthetic Response* (Routledge & Kegan Paul, London and Henley, 1978).

Jakobson, Roman (with Morris Halle), *Fundamentals of Language* (2nd edn, Mouton, The Hague, 1971).

Jauss, Hans Robert, *Toward An Aesthetic of Reception*, trans. Timothy Bahti (Harvester Press, Brighton, 1982).

Jones, Ernest, *Hamlet and Oedipus* (1949; W. W. Norton, New York and London, 1976).

Kristeva, Julia, *The Kristeva Reader*, ed. Toril Moi (Blackwell, Oxford, 1986).

Lacan, Jacques, 'Desire and the Interpretation of Desire in *Hamlet*', *Literature and Psychoanalysis: The Question of Reading: Otherwise, Yale French Studies*, number 55/56, (1980).

Leavis, F. R., *The Common Pursuit* (Chatto & Windus, London, 1953).

Lemon, L. T. and M. J. Reis, eds, *Russian Formalist Criticism: Four Essays* (University of Nebraska Press, Lincoln and London, 1965).

Lévi-Strauss, Claude, *Structuralist Anthropology* (Basic Books, New York, 1963).

Lodge, David, *The Modes of Modern Writing: Metaphor, Metonymy, and the Typology of Modern Literature* (Arnold, London, 1977).

Lukács, Georg, 'The Ideology of Modernism' in *The Meaning of Contemporary Realism*, trans. J. and N. Mander (Merlin Press, London, 1962).

Macherey, Pierre, *A Theory of Literary Production*, trans. G. Wall (Routledge & Kegan Paul, London, Henley and Boston, 1978).

Marx, Karl and Friedrich Engels, *On Literature and Art*, ed. L. Baxandall and S. Morawski (International General, New York, 1974).

Millett, Kate, *Sexual Politics* (Rupert Hart-Davis, London, 1971).

Potter, Lois, *A Preface to Milton* (Longman, London, 1971).

Poulet, Georges, 'Criticism and the Experience of Interiority' in *The Structuralist Controversy*, ed. R. Macksey and E. Donato (Johns Hopkins University Press, Baltimore, 1972), pp. 56–72.

Ruthven, K. K., *Feminist Literary Studies: An Introduction* (Cambridge University Press, Cambridge, 1984).

Saussure, Ferdinand de, *Course in General Linguistics*, trans. Wade Baskin (rev. edn, Fontana, London, 1974).

Selden, Raman, '*King Lear* and "True Need"', *Shakespeare Studies*, vol. 21 (1987), pp. 143–69.

Tillyard, E. M. W., *The Elizabethan World Picture* (Chatto & Windus, London, 1943).

Weber, Max, *The Protestant Ethic and the Spirit of Capitalism*, trans. Talcot Parsons (2nd edn, Allen & Unwin, London, 1976).

Williams, Raymond, *The English Novel from Dickens to Lawrence* (Paladin, London, 1974).

Williams, Raymond, *Marxism and Literature* (Oxford University Press, Oxford, 1977).

Index